THE 99 NAMES OF GOD

Register This New Book

Benefits of Registering*

- ✓ FREE **replacements** of lost or damaged books
- ✓ FREE **audiobook** – *Pilgrim's Progress*, audiobook edition
- ✓ FREE information about new titles and other **freebies**

www.anekopress.com/new-book-registration

*See our website for requirements and limitations.

THE 99 NAMES OF GOD

The "Esmaül-Hüsna"
In the Qur'an and in the Bible

Daniel Wickwire

We love hearing from our readers. Please contact us at www.anekopress.com/questions-comments with any questions, comments, or suggestions.

Visit Daniel's website: www.danwickwire.com
The 99 Names of God – Daniel Wickwire
Copyright © 2018
First edition published 2017
All rights reserved. No part of this book may be reproduced, stored in a retrieval system, or transmitted in any form or by any means – electronic, mechanical, photocopying, recording, or otherwise, without written permission from the publisher.
Scripture taken from the King James Version (KJV), which is in the public domain
Cover Design: J. Martin
Cover Image: Alex_Bond/Shutterstock
eBook Icon: Icons Vector/Shutterstock
Editor: Sheila Wilkinson

Printed in the United States of America
Aneko Press
www.anekopress.com
Aneko Press, Life Sentence Publishing, and our logos are trademarks of
Life Sentence Publishing, Inc.
203 E. Birch Street
P.O. Box 652
Abbotsford, WI 54405

RELIGION / Islam / Theology
Paperback ISBN: 978-1-62245-524-9
eBook ISBN: 978-1-62245-525-6
10 9 8 7 6 5 4 3 2 1
Available where books are sold

Contents

The Esmaül-Hüsna 1	El-Hakk: (51) 32
El-Adl: (29) 4	El-Halik: (11) 33
El-Afuv: (82) 5	El-Halim: (32) 34
El-Ahad: (67) 6	El-Hamid: (56) 35
El-Ahir: (74) 7	El-Hasib: (40) 36
El-Ali: (36) 8	El-Hayy: (62) 37
El-Alim: (19) 9	El-Jami: (87) 38
El-Azim: (33) 10	El-Jebbar: (9) 39
El-Aziz: (8) 11	El-Jelil: (41) 40
El-Ba'is: (49) 12	El-Kabid: (20) 41
El-Baki: (96) 13	El-Kadir: (69) 42
El-Bari: (12) 14	El-Kahhar: (15) 43
El-Basir: (27) 15	El-Kavi: (53) 44
El-Basit: (21) 16	El-Kayyum: (63) 45
El-Batin: (76) 17	El-Kebir: (37) 46
El Bedi: (95) 18	El-Kerim: (42) 47
El-Berr: (79) 19	El-Kuddûs: (4) 48
Ed-Darr: (91) 20	El-Latif: (30) 49
El-Evvel: (73) 21	El-Majid: (65) 50
El-Fettah: (18) 22	Malik'ul-Mulk: (84) 51
El-Ghaffar: (14) 23	El-Mani: (90) 52
El-Ghafur: (34) 24	El-Mejid: (48) 53
El-Ghaniy: (88) 25	El-Melik: (3) 54
El-Habir: (31) 26	El-Metin: (54) 55
El-Hadi: (94) 27	El-Muahhir: (72) 56
El-Hafid: (22) 28	El-Mubdi: (58) 57
El-Hafiz: (38) 29	El-Mughni: (89) 58
El-Hakem: (28) 30	El-Muheymin: (7) 59
El-Hakim: (46) 31	El-Muhsi: (57) 60

El-Muhyi: (60)	61	Es-Samed: (68)	86
El-Muksit: (86)	62	Es-Selam: (5)	87
El-Mu'id: (59)	63	Es-Semi: (26)	88
El-Mu'iz: (24)	64	Esh-Shahid: (50)	89
El-Mujib: (44)	65	Esh-Shekur: (35)	90
El-Mukaddim: (71)	66	Et-Tevvab: (80)	91
El-Mukit: (39)	67	El-Vahid: (66)	92
El-Muktedir: (70)	68	El-Vajid: (64)	93
El-Mu'min: (6)	69	El-Vali: (77)	94
El-Mumit: (61)	70	El-Varis: (97)	95
El-Muntekim: (81)	71	El-Vasi: (45)	96
El-Musavvir: (13)	72	El-Vedud: (47)	97
El-Mute'ali: (78)	73	El-Vehhab: (16)	98
El-Mutekebbir: (10)	74	El-Vekil: (52)	99
El-Muzil: (25)	75	El-Veli: (55)	100
En-Nafi': (92)	76	Ez-Zahir: (75)	101
En-Nur: (93)	77	Zül'-Jelal-i ve'l-Ikram: (85)	102
Er-Rafi: (23)	78	The "Best Names of God" (Esmaül-Hüsna) Mentioned in the Qur'an	103
Er-Rahim: (2)	79		
Er-Rahmân: (1)	80		
Er-Rakib: (43)	81	Index of References Quoted From the Bible	106
Er-Ra'uf: (83)	82		
Er-Reshid: (98)	83	Index of References Quoted From the Qur'an	111
Er-Rezzak: (17)	84		
Es-Sabur: (99)	85		

The Esmaül-Hüsna

The following is an alphabetical list of the names of God. The numbers in parentheses are the typical numbers used in the ordering of the Esmaül-Hüsna – the "most beautiful names."

1. El-Adl: (29) The Just
2. El-Afuv: (82) The Pardoner
3. El-Ahad: (67) The One
4. El-Ahir: (74) The Last
5. El-Ali: (36) The Highest
6. El-Alim: (19) The Omniscient
7. El-Azim: (33) The Magnificent
8. El-Aziz: (8) The Mighty
9. El-Ba'is: (49) The Resurrector
10. El-Baki: (96) The Everlasting
11. El-Bari: (12) The Maker
12. El Basir: (27) The Seer
13. El-Basit: (21) The Enlarger
14. El-Batin: (76) The Hidden
15. El-Bedi: (95) The Originator
16. El-Berr: (79) The Beneficent
17. Ed-Darr: (91) The Afflicter
18. El-Evvel: (73) The First
19. El-Fettah: (18) The Opener
20. El-Ghaffar: (14) The Forgiver
21. El-Ghafur: (34) The Forgiving
22. El-Ghaniy: (88) The Rich
23. El-Habir: (31) The Aware
24. El-Hadi: (94) The Guide
25. El-Hafid: (22) The Abaser
26. El-Hafiz: (38) The Preserver
27. El-Hakem: (28) The Judge
28. El-Hakim: (46) The Wise

29. El-Hakk:	(51) The Truth
30. El-Halik:	(11) The Creator
31. El-Halim:	(32) The Forbearing
32. El-Hamid:	(56) The Praiseworthy
33. El-Hasib:	(40) The Reckoner
34. El-Hayy:	(62) The Living
35. El-Jami:	(87) The Gatherer
36. El-Jebbar:	(9) The Compeller
37. El-Jelil:	(41) The Majestic
38. El-Kabid:	(20) The Withholder
39. El-Kadir:	(69) The Omnipotent
40. El-Kahhar:	(15) The Dominator
41. El-Kavi:	(53) The Strong
42. El-Kayyum:	(63) The Self-Subsisting
43. El-Kebir:	(37) The Greatest
44. El-Kerim:	(42) The Generous
45. El-Kuddus:	(4) The Holy
46. El-Latif:	(30) The Subtle
47. El-Majid:	(65) The Honorable
48. Malik-ul-Mulk:	(84) The Owner of Everything
49. El-Mani:	(90) The Preventer
50. El-Mejid:	(48) The Glorious
51. El-Melik:	(3) The King
52. El-Metin:	(54) The Firm
53. El-Mu'ahhkir:	(72) The Delayer
54. El-Mubdi:	(58) The Originator
55. El-Mughni:	(89) The Enricher
56. El-Muheymin:	(7) The Protector
57. El-Muhsi:	(57) The Numberer
58. El-Muhyi:	(60) The Life-giver
59. El-Muksit:	(86) The Equitable
60. El-Mu'id:	(59) The Restorer
61. El-Mu'iz:	(24) The Honorer
62. El-Mujib:	(44) The Responder
63. El-Mukaddim:	(71) The Expediter
64. El-Mukit:	(39) The Sustainer

65. El-Muktedir:	(70) The Dominant
66. El-Mu'min:	(6) The Faithful
67. El-Mumit:	(61) The Death-giver
68. El-Muntekim:	(81) The Avenger
69. El-Musavvir:	(13) The Designer
70. El-Mute'ali:	(78) The Exalted
71. El-Mutekebir:	(10) The Proud
72. El-Muzil:	(25) The Humbler
73. En-Nafi:	(92) The Blesser
74. En-Nur:	(93) The Light
75. Er-Rafi:	(23) The Exalter
76. Er Rahim:	(2) The Merciful
77. Er-Rahman:	(1) The Compassionate
78. El-Rakib:	(43) The Watchful
79. Er-Ra'uf:	(83) The Kind
80. Er-Reshid:	(98) The Orthodox
81. Er-Rezzak:	(17) The Provider
82. Es-Sabur:	(99) The Patient
83. Es-Samed:	(68) The Eternal
85. Es-Selam:	(5) The Peace
84. Es-Semi:	(26) The Hearer
86. Esh-Shaid:	(50) The Witness
87. Es-Shekur:	(35) The Thankful
88. Et-Tevvab:	(80) The Repentant
89. El-Vahid:	(66) The Unique
90. El-Vajid:	(64) The Discoverer
91. El-Vali:	(77) The Governor
92. El-Varis:	(97) The Inheritor
93. El-Vasi:	(45) The Omnipresent
94. El-Vedud:	(47) The Loving
95. El-Vehhab:	(16) The Bestower
96. El-Vekil:	(52) The Advocate
97. El-Veli:	(55) The Guardian
98. Ez-Zahir:	(75) The Perceptible
99. Zul'-Jelal-i ve'l Ikram:	(85) Lord of Majesty and Honor

1

El-Adl: (29)

(The Just)
(The Righteous One)
His word is perfect in veracity and justice.

Genesis 18:25 – Should not <u>the Judge of all the earth</u> do right?

Deuteronomy 32:4 – *He is* the Rock, his work *is* perfect: for all his ways *are* judgment: a God of truth and without iniquity, just and <u>right *is* he</u>.

Acts 3:14 – But ye denied the Holy One and <u>the Just</u>.

En'am 6:115 – And the word of <u>your Lord</u> has been fulfilled in truth and <u>in justice</u>. None can alter His words, and He is the Hearing, the Knowing.

~~~~~~~~~~~~~~~

Psalm 19:9; Psalm 103:6; Isaiah 45:21; Jeremiah 23:6, 33:16; Acts 7:52; 22:14; 2 Timothy 4:8.
En'am 6:92; A'raf 7:29, 181; Nahl 16:90; Mu'min 40:20.

2

El-Afuv: (82)

(The Pardoner)
He forgives His servants.

Psalm 103:2-3 – (2) Bless the LORD, O my soul, and forget not all his benefits (3) who <u>forgiveth all thine iniquities;</u> and healeth all thy diseases.

Matthew 6:14-15 – (14) For if ye forgive men their trespasses, <u>your heavenly Father will also forgive you</u>: (15) But if ye forgive not men their trespasses, neither will your Father forgive your trespasses.

Hajj 22:60 – That [is so]. And whoever responds [to injustice] with the equivalent of that with which he was harmed and then is tyrannized – Allah will surely aid him. Indeed, <u>Allah is Pardoning and Forgiving</u>.

~~~~~~~~~~~~~~~

Isaiah 43:25; Jeremiah 5:1; Micah 7:18; Acts 3:19; Ephesians 4:32; Colossians 3:13; 1 John 1:9.

3

El-Ahad: (67)

(The One)
There is none other besides Him.

Deuteronomy 6:4 – Hear, O Israel: The LORD <u>our God *is* one LORD</u>.

Zechariah 14:9 – And the LORD shall be king over all the earth: in that day shall there be <u>one LORD</u>, and <u>his name one</u>.

1 Timothy 2:5 – For *there is* <u>one God</u>, and one mediator between God and men, the man Christ Jesus.

James 2:19 – Thou believest that there is <u>one God</u>; thou doest well: the devils also believe, and tremble.

Ikhlas 112:1 – Say, "He is <u>Allah, [who is] One</u>."

~~~~~~~~~~~~~~~

Deuteronomy 4:35, 39; 32:39; 2 Samuel 7:22; Isaiah 43:10-11; Mark 12:29-32; Romans 3:29-30; 1 Corinthians 8:4-6; Galatians 3:20; Ephesians 4:6.

4

El-Ahir: (74)

(The Last)
He is without end.

Isaiah 44:6 – Thus saith the LORD the King of Israel, and his redeemer the LORD of hosts; I am the first, and I *am* the last; and beside me *there is* no God.

Revelation 1:8, 17 – (8) I am Alpha and Omega, the beginning and the ending, saith the Lord, which is, and which was, and which is to come, the Almighty. (17) And when I saw him, I fell at his feet as dead. And he laid his right hand upon me, saying unto me, Fear not; I am the first and the last.

Hadid 57:3 – He is the First and the Last, the Ascendant and the Intimate, and He is, of all things, Knowing.

~~~~~~~~~~~~~~~

Isaiah 41:4; 48:12; Revelation 21:9; 22:13
Rahman 55:26-27.

5

El-Ali: (36)

(The Highest)
(The High and Lofty One)
(The Most High)
He is high and mighty.

1 Chronicles 29:11 – Thine, <u>O LORD, *is* the greatness</u>, and <u>the power</u>, and <u>the glory</u>, and the victory, and <u>the majesty</u>: for all *that is* in the heaven and in the earth *is thine*; thine *is* the kingdom, O LORD, and <u>thou art exalted as head above all</u>.

Mark 5:7 – Jesus, *thou* Son of <u>the most high God</u>? I adjure thee by God, that thou torment me not.

Bakara 2:255 – Allah - there is no deity except Him, the Ever-Living, the Sustainer of [all] existence ... And He is the <u>Most High</u>, the Most Great.

~~~~~~~~~~~~~~~

Numbers 24:16; Deuteronomy 32:8; Luke 1:32, 35, 76.
Bakara 2:29, 32, 115; Nur 22:32.

6

El-Alim: (19)

(The Omniscient)
(The All-Knowing)
He is well aware of everything.

Psalm 139:4 – For *there is* not a word in my tongue, *but*, lo, O LORD, thou knowest it altogether.

John 21:17 – Lord, thou knowest all things ... Jesus saith ... feed my sheep.

Hebrews 4:13 – Neither is there any creature that is not manifest in his sight: but all things are naked and opened unto the eyes of him with whom we have to do.

Bakara 2:115 – And to Allah belongs the east and the west. So wherever you [might] turn, there is the Face of Allah. Indeed, Allah is all-Encompassing and Knowing.

~~~~~~~~~~~~~~~

1 Samuel 2:3; Jeremiah 17:10; Romans 11:33-34; 1 John 3:20. Bakara 2:29, 32, 158; En'am 6:13, 96; Nur 24:32.

7

El-Azim: (33)

(The Magnificent)
(The Mighty Inaccessible)
(The Incomparably Great)
He is high and mighty above all.

Deuteronomy 10:17 – For the LORD your God *is* God of gods, and Lord of lords, <u>a great God</u>.

Jeremiah 32:27 – Behold, I am the LORD, the God of all flesh: <u>is there any thing too hard for me</u>?

Luke 9:43 – They were all amazed at <u>the mighty power of God</u> … at all things which Jesus did.

Bakara 2:255 – Allah - there is no deity except Him, the Ever-Living, the Sustainer of [all] existence. His Kursi extends over the heavens and the earth, and their preservation tires Him not. And He is the Most High, the <u>Most Great</u>.

~~~~~~~~~~~~~~~

1 Chronicles 29:11; Job 4:17; Psalm 92:8; 145:7; Isaiah 1:24.

8

El-Aziz: (8)

(The Mighty)
(The Victorious)
(The Strong)
He is mighty in His sublime sovereignty.

Isaiah 49:26 – And I will feed them that oppress thee with their own flesh ... and all flesh shall know that I the LORD *am* thy Saviour and thy Redeemer, the mighty One of Jacob.

Luke 1:49 – For he that is mighty hath done to me great things; and holy is His name.

Hashr 59:23 – He is Allah, other than whom there is no deity, the King, the Holy, the All-Peaceable, the Bestower of Faith, the Overseer, the Exalted in Might, the Compeller, the Superior. Exalted is Allah above whatever they associate with Him.

~~~~~~~~~~~~~~~

Isaiah 9:6.
Nisa 4:158; Tevbe 9:71.

9

El-Ba'is: (49)

(The Resurrector)
(The Raiser of the Dead)
He will raise up His servants after death
for reward and/or punishment.

Daniel 12:2 – And <u>many</u> of them that sleep in the dust of the earth <u>shall awake</u>, some to everlasting life, and <u>some to shame *and* everlasting contempt</u>.

Acts 26:8 – Why should it be thought a thing incredible with you, that <u>God should raise the dead</u>?

Hajj 22:7 – And [that they may know] that the Hour is coming – no doubt about it – and that <u>Allah will resurrect those in the graves</u>.

~~~~~~~~~~~~~~~~

John 5:21-29; 11:5-44; Acts 4:33; 13:23-38; 1 Corinthians 6:14; 15:15-17, 52-54; 2 Corinthians 1:9; 1 Peter 1:21.

10

El-Baki: (96)

(The Everlasting)
(The Eternal One)
He remains and endures forever.

Deuteronomy 33:27 – The <u>eternal God</u> *is thy* refuge, and underneath *are* the <u>everlasting arms</u>.

Micah 5:2 – But thou, Bethlehem ... out of thee shall he come forth unto me *that is* to be ruler in Israel; whose goings forth *have been* from of old, <u>from everlasting</u>.

Hebrews 13:8 – Jesus Christ the same yesterday, and to day, and <u>for ever</u>.

Taha 20:73 – Indeed, we have believed in our Lord that He may forgive us our sins and what you compelled us [to do] of magic. And <u>Allah is</u> better and <u>more enduring</u>.

~~~~~~~~~~~~~~~

Isaiah 51:6; Psalm 135:13; Micah 5:2; Hebrews 1:11-12; Revelation 1:18.
Hijr 15:23-25; Kasas 28:88; Rahman 55:26-27.

11

El-Bari: (12)

(The Maker)
(The Maker of Order)
(The Rightful Evolver)
We all come from His hand.

Psalm 95:6 – O come, let us worship and bow down: let us kneel before the LORD our maker.

John 1:1-3 – (1) In the beginning was the Word, and the Word was with God, and the Word was God. (3) All things were made by him; and without him was not any thing made that was made.

Hebrews 1:1-2 – (1) God ... (2) hath in these last days spoken unto us by his Son, whom he hath appointed heir of all things, by whom also he made the worlds.

Hashr 59:24 – He is Allah, the Creator, the Inventor, the Fashioner.

~~~~~~~~~~~~~~~

Genesis 1:1, 21, 27; Job 26:13; Isaiah 64:8.
Mulk 67:3.

12

El-Basir: (27)

(The Seer)
(The Observant)
(The All-Seeing)
He sees and hears all things.

Jeremiah 23:24 – Can any hide himself in secret places that I shall not see him? saith the LORD. Do not I fill heaven and earth? saith the LORD.

Hebrews 4:13 – Neither is there any creature that is not manifest in his sight: but all things *are* naked and opened unto the eyes of him with whom we have to do.

Mujadila 58:1 – And Allah hears your dialogue; indeed, Allah is Hearing and Seeing.

~~~~~~~~~~~~~~~

1 Kings 8:39; 1 Chronicles 28:9; 2 Chronicles 16:9;
Job 28:10, 24; Proverbs 5:21; Matthew 6:4; 1 Corinthians 3:20.
Nisa 4:58; Isra 17:1, 30; Hajj 22:61, 75.

13

El-Basit: (21)

(The Enlarger)
(The Spreader and Expander)
He extends His mercy to whom He wills.

2 Samuel 22:37 – <u>Thou hast enlarged my steps</u> under me; so that my feet did not slip.

Psalm 119:32 – I will run the way of thy commandments, when <u>thou shalt enlarge my heart</u>.

John 10:10 – I am come that they might <u>have life</u>, and that they might have *it* <u>more abundantly</u>.

Shura 42:12 – To Him belong the keys of the heavens and the earth. <u>He extends provision</u> for whom He wills and restricts [it].

~~~~~~~~~~~~~~~

Genesis 9:27; 1 Samuel 2:7; 1 Chronicles 4:10;
Psalm 38:2; Isaiah 26:15; Isaiah 54:2; 2 Corinthians 1:8-10;
Ephesians 3:17-19; Revelation 3:7.
Isra 17:30; Ankebut 29:62; Rum 30:37.

14

El-Batin: (76)

(The Hidden)
(The Imperceptible)
He is hidden and screened from the senses;
He is immanent within all things.

Exodus 33:20 – And he said, Thou canst not see my face: for there shall no man see me, and live.

1 Timothy 6:16 – Who only hath immortality, dwelling in the light which no man can approach unto; whom no man hath seen, nor can see: to whom be honour and power everlasting. Amen.

Hadid 57:3 – He is the First and the Last and the Outward and the Inward, and He is Knower of all things.

~~~~~~~~~~~~~~~

Job 11:7; 24:1; 23:8-9; Psalm 145:3; John 1:18;
Romans 1:20; 11:33; Ephesians 3:8; Colossians 1:15, 26;
1 Timothy 1:17.

15

El Bedi: (95)

(The Originator)
(The Inventor)
(The Creative One)
He is incomparably new and unique in creativity.

Psalm 19:1 – <u>The heavens declare the glory of God</u>; and <u>the firmament sheweth his handywork</u>.

John 7:46 – The officers answered, <u>Never man spake like this man</u>.

2 Corinthians 5:17 – Therefore if any man *be* in Christ, <u>*he is* a new creature</u>: old things are passed away; behold, <u>all things are become new</u>.

En'am 6:101 – [He is] Originator of the heavens and the earth. How could He have a son when He does not have a companion and He created all things? And He is, of all things, Knowing.

~~~~~~~~~~~~~~~

Nehemiah 9:6; Matthew 7:28-29; Galatians 6:15.
Bakara 2:117.

16

El-Berr: (79)

(The Beneficent)
(The Doer of Good)
His liberality appears in all His works.

Psalm 25:8 – <u>Good and upright is the LORD</u>: therefore will he teach sinners in the way.

Romans 2:4 – Or despisest thou the riches of <u>his goodness</u> and forbearance and longsuffering; not knowing that <u>the goodness of God</u> leadeth thee to repentance?

James 1:5 – If any of you lack wisdom, let him ask of <u>God</u>, that <u>giveth to all *men* liberally</u>, and upbraideth not; and it shall be given him.

Tur 52:28 – Indeed, we used to supplicate Him before. Indeed, it is He who is <u>the Beneficent</u>, the Merciful.

~~~~~~~~~~~~~~~~

Exodus 34:6-7; Psalm 119:68; John 10:10; Romans 11:22; Titus 3:4-6.

17

Ed-Darr: (91)

(The Afflicter)
(The Creator of the Harmful)
He sends affliction as well as blessing.

Psalm 55:19 – <u>God shall</u> hear, and <u>afflict them</u>, even he that abideth of old. Selah. Because they have no changes, therefore they fear not God.

Lamentations 3:33 – <u>For he doth not afflict willingly</u> nor grieve the children of men.

Romans 11:22 – <u>Behold</u> therefore the goodness and <u>severity of God</u>: on them which fell, severity; but toward thee, goodness, if thou continue in *his* goodness: otherwise thou also shalt be cut off.

Fetih 48:11 – Say, "Then <u>who could prevent Allah at all if He intended for you harm</u> or intended for your benefit?"

~~~~~~~~~~~~~~

Ruth 1:21; Zephaniah 1:17.
En'am 6:17.

18

El-Evvel: (73)

(The First)
He was before the beginning.

Isaiah 44:6 – Thus saith the LORD the King of Israel, and his redeemer the LORD of hosts; I am the first, and I *am* the last; and beside me *there is* no God.

Revelation 1:17-18 – (17) And when I saw him, I fell at his feet as dead. And he laid his right hand upon me, saying unto me, Fear not; I am the first and the last: (18) *I am* he that liveth, and was dead; and, behold, I am alive for evermore, Amen; and have the keys of hell and of death.

―――――――――

Hadid 57:3 – He is the First and the Last, the Ascendant and the Intimate, and He is, of all things, Knowing.

~~~~~~~~~~~~~~~

Micah 5:2; John 1:1-3; Hebrews 13:8;
Revelation 1:8, 11; 2:8; 21:6; 22:13.

19

El-Fettah: (18)

(The Opener)
(The Victory Giver)
(The Judge)
He clears and opens up the Way.

Revelation 3:7-8 – (7) These things saith he that is holy, he that is true ... <u>he that openeth</u>, and no man shutteth; and shutteth, and no man openeth; (8) I know thy works: <u>behold, I have set before thee an open door</u>, and no man can shut it.

John 10:7-11 – (9) <u>I am the door</u>: <u>by me</u> if any man <u>enter in</u>, he shall be saved, and shall go in and out, and find pasture.

Sebe 34:26 – Say, "<u>Our Lord will bring us together</u>; then He will judge between us in truth. And He is the Knowing Judge."

~~~~~~~~~~~~~~~

Isaiah 3:13; Luke 24:32, 45; Acts 10:42; 1 Timothy 2:5; Revelation 5:2-9.

20

El-Ghaffar: (14)

(The Forgiver)
(The Indulgent One)
He is ever ready to pardon and forgive.

Nehemiah 9:17 – And refused to obey, neither were mindful of thy wonders that thou didst among them; but hardened their necks, and in their rebellion appointed a captain to return to their bondage: but thou *art* <u>a God ready to pardon</u>, gracious and merciful, slow to anger, and of great kindness, and forsookest them not.

Taha 20:82 – But indeed, I am <u>the Perpetual Forgiver</u> of whoever repents and believes and does righteousness and then continues in guidance.

~~~~~~~~~~~~~~~

Exodus 34:6-7; 2 Chronicles 7:14; Isaiah 55:7;
Matthew 6:14-15; Matthew 9:2, 5; Luke 5:20; 1 John 1:9.
Nuh 71:10.

21

El-Ghafur: (34)

(The Forgiving)
(The Forgiver of Faults)
He forgives and pardons.

Exodus 34:6-7 – (6) The LORD, The LORD God, merciful and gracious, longsuffering, and abundant in goodness and truth, (7) Keeping mercy for thousands, <u>forgiving iniquity and transgression and sin</u>.

Luke 5:19-21 – (20) When he [Jesus] saw their faith, he said unto him, Man, <u>thy sins are forgiven</u> thee. (21) … Who is this which speaketh blasphemies? <u>Who can forgive sins, but God alone</u>?

Enfal 8:69 – So consume what you have taken of war booty [as being] lawful and good, and fear Allah. Indeed, <u>Allah is Forgiving</u> and Merciful.

~~~~~~~~~~~~~~~

Nehemiah 9:17; Isaiah 55:7; Mark 2:10-12.
Bakara 2:173, 225; Al-i Imran 3:155; Maide 5:3; Nahl 16:110.

22

El-Ghaniy: (88)

(The Rich)
(The Independently Wealthy One)
(The Self-Sufficient One)
He is free from all wants and needs; He possesses all.

Proverbs 8:18 – <u>Riches</u> and honour *are* <u>with me</u>; *yea*, durable riches and righteousness.

Ephesians 2:4-7 – (4) But <u>God</u>, <u>who is rich in mercy</u>, for his great love wherewith he loved us … (7) That in the ages to come he might shew <u>the exceeding riches of his grace</u> in his kindness toward us through Christ Jesus.

Bakara 2:267 – And know that <u>Allah is Free of need</u> and Praiseworthy.

~~~~~~~~~~~~~~~~

1 Chronicles 29:12; Psalm 50:12; Isaiah 66:1;
2 Corinthians 8:9.
Bakara 2:263; Al-i İmran 3:97; Zumar 39:7; Muhammad 47:38; Hadid 57:24.

23

El-Habir: (31)

(The Aware)
(The Well Informed One)
He is wise and aware of all.

Job 28:24 – For <u>he looketh to the ends of the earth</u>, *and* <u>seeth under the whole heaven</u>.

Psalm 139:1-4 – (1) <u>O LORD</u>, thou hast searched me, and known *me*. (2) ... <u>thou understandest my thought afar off</u> ... (4) For there *is* not a word in my tongue, *but*, lo, <u>O LORD, thou knowest it altogether</u>.

Acts 1:24 – Thou, <u>Lord, which knowest the hearts of all</u> *men*.

Ahzab 33:34 – And remember what is recited in your houses of the verses of Allah and wisdom. Indeed, <u>Allah is</u> ever Subtle and <u>Acquainted [with all things]</u>.

~~~~~~~~~~~~~~

Psalm 147:5; Matthew 10:30; Romans 11:33-36; Hebrews 4:13; 1 John 3:19-20.
Bakara 2:271; Nisa 4:35; En'am 6:18, 73; Hud 11:1.

24

El-Hadi: (94)

(The Guide)
(The Way)
He leads and guides in safe paths.

Psalm 48:14 – For this God is our God for ever and ever: <u>he will be our guide even unto death</u>.

John 16:13 – Howbeit when he, <u>the Spirit</u> of truth, is come, he <u>will guide you</u> into all truth.

Hajj 22:54 – And so those who were given knowledge may know that it is the truth from your Lord and [therefore] believe in it, and their hearts humbly submit to it. And indeed is <u>Allah the Guide</u> of those who have believed to a straight path.

~~~~~~~~~~~~~~~~

Psalm 17:6; 23:2-3; 25:4, 9-10; 32:8; 37:23; 48:14; Proverbs 1:33; 3:5-6; 4:18; 16:9; 20:24; Isaiah 26:7; 58:11; Jeremiah 6:16; 29:11; John 8:12; John 14:6; John 16:13.

25

El-Hafid: (22)

(The Abaser)
(The Humbler)
He abases some while He exalts others.

Ezekiel 21:26 – Thus saith the Lord GOD; Remove the diadem, and take off the crown: this *shall* not *be* the same: exalt *him that is* low, and <u>abase *him that is* high</u>.

Matthew 23:12 – And whosoever shall exalt himself <u>shall be abased</u>; and he that shall humble himself shall be exalted.

Vakia 56:1-3 – (1) When the Occurrence occurs, (2) There is, at its occurrence, no denial. (3) <u>It will bring down [some]</u> and raise up [others].

~~~~~~~~~~~~~~~

Deuteronomy 8:2, 16; Isaiah 2:12; Isaiah 23:9; Ezekiel 21:26; Daniel 4:37; Luke 18:14; James 4:6; 1 Peter 5:5-6 / Tin 95:5.

26

El-Hafiz: (38)

(The Preserver)
(The Guardian)
He keeps watch over everything.

Psalm 121:5-8 – (5) <u>The Lord is thy keeper</u> … (7) <u>The LORD shall preserve thee</u> from all evil: he shall preserve thy soul. (8) <u>The LORD shall preserve</u> thy going out and thy coming in from this time forth, and even for evermore.

John 10:28 – And I give unto them eternal life; and <u>they shall never perish</u>, neither shall any *man* pluck them out of my hand.

Sebe 34:21 – And he had over them no authority except [it was decreed] that We might make evident who believes in the Hereafter from who is thereof in doubt. And <u>your Lord, over all things, is Guardian</u>.

~~~~~~~~~~~~~~~~

Job 7:20; Psalm 212:8; Jeremiah 31:28; 1 Peter 1:5.
Hud 11:57.

27

El-Hakem: (28)

(The Judge)
He settles all disputes.

Psalm 96:13 – Before <u>the LORD</u>: for he cometh, for he <u>cometh to judge the earth</u>: <u>he shall judge the world</u> with righteousness, and the people with his truth.

John 5:22 – For the Father judgeth no man, but hath committed <u>all judgment unto the Son</u>.

Hebrews 12:23 – To the general assembly and church of the firstborn, which are written in heaven, and to <u>God the Judge of all</u>, and to the spirits of just men made perfect.

Tin 95:8 – Is not <u>Allah the most just of judges</u>?

~~~~~~~~~~~~~~~

Genesis 18:25; Deuteronomy 32:36; Acts 10:39-42;
2 Timothy 4:1; 1 Peter 4:5; Revelation 19:11.
Hajj 22:69; Mu'min 40:48.

28

El-Hakim: (46)

(The Wise)
He perfectly knows all things.

Daniel 2:20-21 – (20) Blessed be the name of God for ever and ever: for <u>wisdom</u> and might <u>are his</u>: (21) ... <u>he giveth wisdom</u> unto the wise, <u>and knowledge</u> to them that know understanding.

Jude 1:25 – To <u>the only wise God</u> our Saviour, *be* glory and majesty, dominion and power, both now and ever. Amen.

Bakara 2:129 – Our Lord, and send among them a messenger from themselves who will recite to them Your verses and <u>teach them the Book and wisdom</u> and purify them. Indeed, <u>You are</u> the Exalted in Might, <u>the Wise</u>.

~~~~~~~~~~~~~~~

Psalm 147:5; Colossians 2:3.
Bakara 2:32, 228, 240; Al-i İmran 3:6; Nisa 4:17; En'am 6:73; Fussilet 41:42.

29

El-Hakk: (51)

(The Truth)
(The True One)
He really exists as the One who is genuine and true.

Jeremiah 10:10 – But the LORD *is* the true God, he *is* the living God, and an everlasting king: at his wrath the earth shall tremble, and the nations shall not be able to abide his indignation.

John 14:6, 17 – (6) Jesus saith unto him, I am the way, the truth, and the life: no man cometh unto the Father, but by me. (17) Even the Spirit of truth whom the world cannot receive, because it seeth him not, neither knoweth him.

Hakka 69:1 – The Reality!

~~~~~~~~~~~~~~~

Numbers 23:19; Isaiah 25:1.
Al-i İmran 3:60; En'am 6:62; Yunus 10:108; Hajj 22:62; Mu'minun 23:116; Nur 24:25; Luqman 31:30;

30

El-Halik: (11)

(The Creator)
He brought all things from non-existence into existence.

Isaiah 40:28 – Hast thou not known? hast thou not heard, that the everlasting God, the LORD, the Creator of the ends of the earth, fainteth not, neither is weary?

Revelation 4:11 – O Lord … thou hast created all things, and for thy pleasure they are and were created.

Hashr 59:24 – He is Allah, the Creator, the Inventor, the Fashioner; to Him belong the best names. Whatever is in the heavens and earth is exalting Him. And He is the Exalted in Might, the Wise.

~~~~~~~~~~~~~~~

Genesis 1:1; Ecclesiastes 12:1; Colossians 1:3-16; 1 Peter 4:9. En'am 6:102; Ra'd 13:16; Zumar 39:62.

31

El-Halim: (32)

(The Forbearing)
(The Meek and Lowly One)
He is both forgiving and kindly disposed.

Zechariah 9:9 – Behold, <u>thy King</u> cometh unto thee: he is just, and having salvation; <u>lowly</u>, and riding upon an ass, and upon a colt the foal of an ass.

Matthew 21:1-11 – (5) Behold, <u>thy King</u> cometh unto thee, <u>meek</u>, and sitting upon an ass.

Romans 2:4 – Or despisest thou the riches of his goodness and <u>forbearance and longsuffering</u>; not knowing that the goodness <u>of God</u> leadeth thee to repentance?

Bakara 2:225 – Allah does not impose blame upon you for what is unintentional in your oaths … And <u>Allah is</u> Forgiving and <u>Forbearing</u>.

~~~~~~~~~~~~~~

Matthew 11:28-30; Galatians 5:22-23.
Maide 5:101; Isra 17:44; Hajj 22:59.

32

El-Hamid: (56)

(The Praiseworthy)
(The Praised One)
(The All-Praised)
He is worthy of all praise and adoration.

Psalm 48:1 – A Song *and* Psalm for the sons of Korah. Great is <u>the LORD,</u> and <u>greatly to be praised</u> in the city of our God, *in* the mountain of his holiness.

Revelation 19:5 – And a voice came out of the throne, saying, <u>Praise our God,</u> all ye his servants, and ye that fear him, both small and great.

Bakara 2:267 – And know that *<u>Allah is</u>* Free of need and <u>Praiseworthy</u>.

~~~~~~~~~~~~~~~

Psalm 9:11; 34:1; 50:23; 96:4; 100:4; 119:164; Hebrews 13:15;
2 Peter 2:9; Revelation 5:13.
Hud 11:73; Ibrahim 14:72; Hajj 22:4, 24; Lokman 31:26;
Fatir 35:15.

33

El-Hasib: (40)

(The Reckoner)
(The Accounter)
(The One Who Brings Judgment)
He is sufficient as a reckoner.

Malachi 3:8-10 – (8) <u>Will a man rob God</u>? Yet ye have robbed me. But ye say, Wherein have we robbed thee? In tithes and offerings. (9) Ye *are* cursed with a curse: for ye have robbed me, *even* this whole nation.

Romans 14:12 – So then, <u>each of us will give an account of himself to God</u>.

Nisa 4:86 – And when you are greeted with a greeting, greet [in return] with one better than it or [at least] return it [in a like manner]. Indeed, <u>Allah is</u> ever, over all things, <u>an Accountant</u>.

~~~~~~~~~~~~~~~

Matthew 10:30; 12:36; Acts 5:1-11; 2 Corinthians 5:10.
Nisa 4:6-7.

34

El-Hayy: (62)

(The Living)
(The Ever-Living One)
(The Alive)
He is the source of all life.

Jeremiah 10:10 – But the LORD *is* the true God, he *is* the living God, and an everlasting king. (Elohim Chaiyim)

Acts 3:15 – And killed the Prince of life, whom God hath raised from the dead; whereof we are witnesses.

John 1:4 – In him was life; and the life was the light of men.

Bakara 2:255 – Allah – there is no deity except Him, the Ever-Living, the Sustainer of [all] existence.

~~~~~~~~~~~~~~~

Psalm 36:9; 84:2; John 1:4; 5:26; 6:51; 7:37-39; 14:6; Hebrews 4:12; 9:14; 10:31; Revelation 1:18.
Al-i İmran 3:2; TaHa 20:111; Furkan 25:58; Mu'min 40:65.

35

El-Jami: (87)

(The Gatherer)
He gathers all men to an appointed Day.

Isaiah 66:18 – For I know their works and their thoughts: it shall come, that <u>I will gather all nations</u> and tongues; and they shall come, and see my glory.

Matthew 24:31 – And he shall send his angels with a great sound of a trumpet, and <u>they shall gather together his elect</u> from the four winds, from one end of heaven to the other.

Al-i İmran 3:9 – <u>Our Lord</u>, surely <u>You will gather the people for a Day</u> about which there is no doubt. Indeed, Allah does not fail in His promise.

~~~~~~~~~~~~~~~

Psalm 50:5; Jeremiah 23:3; 29:14; Matthew 13:41; 24:31; 25:32; Luke 13:34-35; John 10:16; 11:52; Ephesians 1:10; Revelation 20:8.

36

El-Jebbar: (9)

(The Compeller)
(The All Powerful One)
His will is always done, and His might
and power are absolute.

Jeremiah 32:17, 27 – (17) Ah Lord GOD! behold, thou hast made the heaven and the earth by thy great power and stretched out arm, *and* there is nothing too hard for thee: (27) Behold, I *am* the LORD, the God of all flesh: is there any thing too hard for me?

2 Corinthians 5:14 – For Christ's love constraineth us; because we thus judge, that if one died for all, then were all dead.

Hashr 59:23 – He is Allah, other than whom there is no deity, the King, the Holy, the All-Peaceable, the Bestower of Faith, the Overseer, the Exalted in Might, the Compeller.

~~~~~~~~~~~~~~~

Job 42:2; Matthew 19:26.

37

El-Jelil: (41)

(The Majestic)
(The Beneficent)
(The Sublime)
(The Mighty)
(The Revered)
(The Glorious One)
He alone is mighty and great.

Daniel 7:14 – And <u>there was given him dominion, and glory</u>, and a kingdom, that all people, nations, and languages, should serve him: his dominion *is* an everlasting dominion, which shall not pass away, and his kingdom that which shall not be destroyed.

John 2:11 – This beginning of miracles did Jesus in Cana of Galilee, and <u>manifested forth his glory</u>.

Rahman 55:27 – And there will remain the Face of <u>your Lord, Owner of Majesty</u> and Honor.

~~~~~~~~~~~~~~~

Exodus 15:6; Psalm 145:5; Acts 7:55.
A'raf 7:143; Zumar 39:14.

38

El-Kabid: (20)

(The Withholder)
(The Restrainer or Retainer)
(The Constrictor or Restrictor)
He squeezes and puts the pressure on.

Ezekiel 31:15 – Thus says the Lord GOD, In the day when it went down to the grave I caused a mourning: <u>I closed the deep</u> for him and I <u>restraimed the floods thereof</u>.

2 Peter 2:16 – But was rebuked for his iniquity: the dumb ass speaking with man's voice <u>forbad the madness of the prophet</u>.

Bakara 2:245 – Who is it that would loan Allah a goodly loan so He may multiply it for him many times over? And <u>it is Allah who withholds</u> and grants abundance, and to Him you will be returned.

~~~~~~~~~~~~~~~

Exodus 36:6; 2 Kings 19:28; Ezekiel 31:15; Matthew 26:52-53; Mark 13:20; Luke 8:22-25.

39

El-Kadir: (69)

(The Omnipotent)
(The All-Powerful)
(The Mighty)
He is able to do what He pleases.

Jeremiah 32:17 – Ah <u>Lord GOD</u>! behold, thou hast made the heaven and the earth by thy great power and stretched out arm, *and* <u>there is nothing too hard for thee</u>:

Revelation 19:6 – Alleluia: for <u>the Lord God omnipotent reigneth</u>.

Fatir 35:44 – <u>Allah is not to be caused failure</u> by anything in the heavens or on the earth. Indeed, for <u>He is</u> the Wise and <u>the Mighty</u>.

~~~~~~~~~~~~~~~

Genesis 17:1; Job 37:23; 42:2; Psalm 147:5; Isaiah 40:13; John 10:17-18; Romans 1:20; Hebrews 1:3.
Bakara 2:20 & 284; Maide 5:17; En'am 6:65; Tevbe 9:39; Fatir 35:44; Ya-Sin 36:81; Ahkaf 46:33; Kiyamah 75:40.

40

El-Kahhar: (15)

(The Dominator)
(The One Who Subdues)
(The Subduer)
He powerfully avenges and overcomes all.

Psalm 47:2-3 – (2) For the LORD most high *is* terrible; *he is* a great King over all the earth. (3) <u>He shall subdue the people</u> under us, and the nations under our feet.

2 Thessalonians 1:8 – In flaming fire <u>taking vengeance on them that know not God</u>, and that obey not the gospel of our Lord Jesus Christ.

Mu'min 40:16 – The Day they come forth nothing concerning them will be concealed from Allah. To whom belongs [all] sovereignty this Day? To <u>Allah</u>, the One, the <u>Prevailing</u>.

~~~~~~~~~~~~~~~

Psalm 94:1; Romans 3:5.
Yusuf 12:39; Ra'd 13:16-17; Sad 38:65.

41

El-Kavi: (53)

(The Strong)
(The Most Powerful One)
(The Possessor of All Strength)
He is sublime in His strength and His power.

Psalm 24:8 – Who is this King of glory? The LORD, <u>strong and mighty</u>, the LORD, <u>mighty in battle</u>.

Revelation 19:6 – And I heard as it were the voice of a great multitude, and as the voice of many waters, and as the voice of mighty thunderings, saying, Alleluia: for <u>the Lord God omnipotent reigneth</u>.

Hud 11:66 – Indeed, it is your Lord who is <u>the Powerful, the Exalted in Might</u>.

~~~~~~~~~~~~~~~

Exodus 6:1; Psalm 89:8; Isaiah 40:25-31; Matthew 28:18; Luke 1:49, 51; 3:16; 1 Corinthians 1:25; Revelation 15:3; 21:22. Hajj 22:40, 74; Shura 42:19; Hadid 57:25; Mujadala 58:21.

42

El-Kayyum: (63)

(The Self-Subsisting)
(The Self-Existing by Whom All Subsist)
He is eternally existing in and for Himself alone.

Exodus 3:14-15 – (14) And <u>God</u> said unto Moses, <u>I AM THAT I AM</u>: and he said, Thus shalt thou say unto the children of Israel, <u>I AM</u> hath sent me unto you. (15) … <u>This *is* my name for ever</u>, and this *is* my memorial unto all generations.

1 Timothy 6:14-16 – (14) Our <u>Lord Jesus Christ</u> … (16) <u>Who only hath immortality</u>, dwelling in the light which no man can approach.

Al-i İmran 3:2 – Allah – there is no deity except Him, the Ever-Living, <u>the Sustainer of existence</u>.

~~~~~~~~~~~~~~~

Exodus 6:3; Psalm 90:2; 102:27; Isaiah 57:15;
Hebrews 1:2; 11:3.
Bakara 2:255; Taha 20:111.

43

El-Kebir: (37)

(The Greatest)
(The Most Great One)
He is able to subdue all unto Himself.

Deuteronomy 10:17 – For the LORD your God *is* <u>God of gods</u>, and Lord of lords, <u>a great God</u>, a mighty, and a terrible.

Luke 1:32, 35 – (32) <u>He shall be great</u>, and shall be called the Son of the Highest. (35) The Holy Ghost shall come upon thee, and the power of the Highest shall overshadow thee: therefore also that holy thing which shall be born of thee shall be called the Son of God.

Hajj 22:62 – That is because Allah is the Truth, and that which they call upon other than Him is falsehood, and because Allah is the Most High, the Grand.

~~~~~~~~~~~~~~

Job 33:12; Philippians 2:10.
Ra'd 13:9; Lokman 31:30; Sebe 34:23.

44

El-Kerim: (42)

(The Generous)
(The Munificent)
(The Bountiful Noble One)
He is liberal in His generosity.

Psalm 116:7 – Return unto thy rest, O my soul; for the LORD hath dealt <u>bountifully</u> with thee.

James 1:5 – If any of you lack wisdom, let him ask of God, that giveth to all *men* <u>liberally</u>, and upbraideth not; and it shall be given him.

Neml 27:40 – And whoever is grateful – his gratitude is only for [the benefit of] himself. And whoever is ungrateful – then indeed, <u>my Lord is</u> Free of need and <u>Generous</u>.

~~~~~~~~~~~~~~~

Genesis 24:35; Numbers 14:8; Deuteronomy 28:11; Psalm 65:9-13; 117:2; Isaiah 54:8, 10; Jeremiah 33:6-9; Matthew 7:11; Acts 14:17; Romans 11:35-36.

45

El-Kuddûs: (4)

(The Holy)
(The Most Perfect Pure One)
He is pure from imperfection.

Isaiah 6:3 – Holy, holy, holy, is the LORD of hosts: *(Elohim Kedoshim)*

Luke 1:35, 46-49 – (35) The Holy Ghost shall come upon thee … (46) My soul doth magnify the Lord … (47) God my Saviour … (49) Holy is his name.

Acts 2:27 – Because thou wilt not leave my soul in hell, neither wilt thou suffer thine Holy One to see corruption.

Juma 62:1 – Whatever is in the heavens and in the earth glorifies Allah, the Sovereign, the Holy One, the Mighty, the Wise.

~~~~~~~~~~~~~~~

Leviticus 19:2; Psalm 99:5; Habakkuk 1:12; John 17:11; Acts 3:14; Hebrews 7:26; 1 Peter 1:15-16; Revelation 4:8. Hashr 59:23.

46

El-Latif: (30)

(The Subtle)
(The Benevolent One)
(The Gentle)
His kind grace extends to all His servants.

Exodus 34:6-7 – (6) The LORD, <u>The LORD</u> <u>God, merciful and gracious</u>, longsuffering, and abundant in goodness and truth, (7) Keeping mercy for thousands, forgiving iniquity and transgression and sin, and that will by no means clear *the guilty*.

Titus 2:11 – For <u>the grace of God</u> that bringeth salvation hath appeared to all men...

En'am 6:103 – Vision perceives Him not, but He perceives [all] vision; and He is <u>the Subtle</u>, the Acquainted.

~~~~~~~~~~~~~~~

Psalm 117:2; Isaiah 54:8-10; Romans 2:4-5; 9:22; 1 Peter 3:20; 2 Peter 3:9.
Hajj 22:63; Lokman 31:16; Shura 42:19; Mulk 67:14.

47

El-Majid: (65)

(The Honorable)
(The Noble)
(The High and Glorious One)
He is praiseworthy and all glorious.

1 Samuel 2:30 – But now the LORD saith, Be it far from me; for them that <u>honour me</u> I will honour, and they that despise me shall be lightly esteemed.

Revelation 4:11 – Thou art worthy, O Lord, to receive glory and <u>honour</u> and power: for thou hast created all things, and for thy pleasure they are and were created.

Buruj 85:15 – <u>Honorable</u> Owner of the Throne.

~~~~~~~~~~~~~~~

1 Chronicles 16:25-27; 29:11-12; Psalm 22:23; 29:2; 57:5; 111:3; 145:5; Daniel 4:34; John 5:23; 8:54; Philippians 2:9-11; Revelation 19:7.

48

Malik'ul-Mulk: (84)

(The Owner of Everything)
(King Over Every Earthly Kingdom)
He reigns in complete sovereignty over the world.

Psalm 24:1 – <u>The earth *is* the LORD'S</u>, and the fulness thereof; the world, and they that dwell therein.

1 Timothy 1:17 – Now unto <u>the King eternal</u>, immortal, invisible, the only wise God, *be* honour and glory for ever and ever. Amen.

———————

Al-i İmran 3:26 – Say, "O Allah, <u>Owner of Sovereignty</u>, You give sovereignty to whom You will and You take sovereignty away from whom You will. You honor whom You will and You humble whom You will. In Your hand is [all] good. Indeed, You are over all things competent."

~~~~~~~~~~~~~~~

Deuteronomy 10:14; Exodus 9:29; Psalm 89:11; 95:4-5; 1 Chronicles 29:11; 1 Corinthians 10:26.

49

El-Mani: (90)

(The Preventer)
(The Defender from Harm)
He prohibits, suppresses, and
withholds when He wishes.

Genesis 30:2 – And Jacob's anger was kindled against Rachel: and he said, *Am* I in <u>God's stead, who hath withheld</u> from thee the fruit of the womb?

Acts 16:6-7 – (6) Now when they had gone throughout Phrygia and the region of Galatia, and were forbidden of the Holy Ghost to preach the word in Asia. (7) After they were come to Mysia, they assayed to go into Bithynia: but <u>the Spirit suffered them not</u>.

Note: The word *Mani* is not found in the Qur'an.

~~~~~~~~~~~~~~~

Amos 4:7; Job 12:13; Psalm 84:11; 107:33-34; Malachi 3:11; 2 Corinthians 12:8-9; James 5:17.

50

El-Mejid: (48)

(The Glorious)
(The Grand and Majestic One)
He is worthy of all glory and honor.

Exodus 15:11 – Who *is* like unto thee, O LORD, among the gods? Who *is* like thee, glorious in holiness, fearful *in* praises, doing wonders?

1 Corinthians 2:8 – Which none of the princes of this world knew: for had they known *it*, they would not have crucified the Lord of glory.

Hud 11:73 – They said, "Are you amazed at the decree of Allah? May the mercy of Allah and His blessings be upon you, people of the house. Indeed, He is Praiseworthy and Honorable."

~~~~~~~~~~~~~~~

Deuteronomy 28:58; 1 Chronicles 29:13; Nehemiah 9:5-6; Psalm 72:19; 76:4; 145:5; Matthew 25:31; Acts 7:55; Titus 2:13; Hebrews 1:3; Hebrews 2:9.

51

El-Melik: (3)

(The King)
(The Absolute Ruler)
(The Eternal Lord)
He is King and Sovereign Lord.

Isaiah 43:15 – I *am* the LORD, your Holy One, the creator of Israel, your King.

John 18:36 – Jesus answered, My kingdom is not of this world.

1 Timothy 1:17 – Now unto the King eternal, immortal, invisible, the only wise God, be honour and glory.

Hashr 59:23 – He is Allah, other than whom there is no deity, the King, the Holy, the All-Peaceable, the Bestower of Faith, the Overseer, the Exalted in Might, the Compeller, the Superior. Exalted is Allah above whatever they associate with Him.

~~~~~~~~~~~~~~~

Zechariah 9:9; Luke 23:2-3; 1 Timothy 6:15; Revelation 15:3. Ta-Ha 20:114; Cuma 62:1.

52

El-Metin: (54)

(The Firm)
(The Immovable and Unchanging One)
(The Forceful One)
(The Authoritative One)
He is firm in his possession of strength.

Proverbs 18:10 – The name of the LORD *is* a strong tower: the righteous runneth into it, and is safe.

James 1:17 – Every good gift and every perfect gift is from above, and cometh down from the Father of lights, with whom is no variableness, neither shadow of turning.

Dhariyat 51:58 – Indeed, it is Allah who is the [continual] Provider, the firm possessor of strength.

~~~~~~~~~~~~~~~

1 Kings 8:56; Psalm 33:11; 102:26-27; Isaiah 46:9-10;
2 Timothy 2:19; 1 Corinthians 3:11; Hebrews 13:8.

53

El-Muahhir: (72)

(The Delayer)
He prevents or sends away as He wishes.

Genesis 16:2 – And Sarai said unto Abram, Behold now, <u>the LORD hath restrained me</u> from bearing.

2 Thessalonians 2:6-7 – (6) And now ye know what <u>withholdeth</u> that he might be revealed in his time. (7) For the mystery of iniquity doth already work: only he who now <u>letteth</u> *will let*, until he be taken out of the way.

Ibrahim 14:10, 42 – (10) Can there be doubt about Allah, Creator of the heavens and earth? He invites you that He may forgive you of your sins, and He delays your death for a specified term. (42) <u>He only delays them</u> for a Day when eyes will stare [in horror].

~~~~~~~~~~~~~~~

1 Samuel 14:6; 25:34; Romans 3:25; 2 Peter 2:16; 3:9.

54

El-Mubdi: (58)

(The Originator)
(The Producer)
He both originates and restores.

Isaiah 45:18 – For thus saith the LORD that created the heavens; God himself that formed the earth and made it; he hath established it, he created it not in vain, he formed it to be inhabited: I *am* the LORD; and *there is* none else.

Revelation 4:11 – Thou art worthy, O Lord, to receive glory and honour and power: for thou hast created all things, and for thy pleasure they are and were created.

Buruj 85:13 – Indeed, it is He who originates [creation] and repeats.

~~~~~~~~~~~~~~~

Genesis 1:1, 21, 25, 27; 2:3-4; 5:1-2; Isaiah 40:28; 41:20; John 1:3; Ephesians 3:9; Colossians 1:16; Hebrews 1:1-3; 1 Peter 4:19.

55

El-Mughni: (89)

(The Enricher)
(The Rich)
He provides bounty and supplies others needs.

Proverbs 15:6 – In the house of the righteous *is* <u>much treasure</u>: but in the revenues of the wicked is trouble.

Philippians 4:19 – But my <u>God shall supply all your need</u> according to his riches in glory by Christ Jesus.

Nisa 4:131 – And <u>to Allah belongs whatever is in the heavens and whatever is on the earth</u> ... to Allah belongs whatever is in the heavens and whatever is on the earth. And ever is Allah Free of need and Praiseworthy.

~~~~~~~~~~~~~~~

Psalm 119:72; Isaiah 33:5-6; Romans 2:4;
2 Corinthians 9:10-11; 1 Timothy 6:17.
Tevbe 9:74-75; Huha 93:8.

56

El-Muheymin: (7)

(The Protector)
(The Vigilant One)
(The Guardian)
His watchful care preserves from harm.

Psalm 121:7-8 – (7) The LORD shall preserve thee from all evil: he shall preserve thy soul. (8) The LORD shall preserve thy going out and thy coming in from this time forth, and even for evermore.

2 Timothy 4:18 – And the Lord shall deliver me from every evil work, and will preserve *me* unto his heavenly kingdom: to whom be glory for ever and ever. Amen.

Hashr 59:23 – He is Allah, other than whom there is no deity, the King, the Holy, the All-Peaceable, the Bestower of Faith, the Overseer.

~~~~~~~~~~~~~

Nehemiah 9:6; Psalm 12:7; Proverbs 2:8; John 10:8-11.

57

El-Muhsi: (57)

(The Numberer)
(The Appraiser)
(The Reckoner)
(The Computer)
He has counted and numbered all things.

Job 31:4 – Doth not he see my ways, and count all my steps?

Matthew 10:30 – But the very hairs of your head are all numbered.

Ya Sin 36:12 – Indeed, it is We who bring the dead to life and record what they have put forth and what they left behind, and all things We have enumerated in a clear register.

~~~~~~~~~~~~~~~

Job 14:16; Psalm 147:4-5; Isaiah 40:25-26; Daniel 5:26; Luke 12:7; Revelation 13:8; 20:15.
Meryem 19:94; Mujadala 58:6; Jinn 72:28; Naba 78:29; Infitar 82:10-12.

58

El-Muhyi: (60)

(The Life-giver)
(The Resuscitator)
(The Restorer)
(The Giver of Life)
He quickens and brings to life the dead.

Genesis 2:7 – And the LORD God formed man *of* the dust of the ground, and <u>breathed into his nostrils the breath of life</u>; and man became a living soul.

John 5:21 – For as the Father raiseth up the dead, and quickeneth *them*; even so <u>the Son quickeneth whom he will</u>.

Rum 30:50 – So observe the effects of the mercy of Allah – how <u>He gives life to the earth</u> after its lifelessness. Indeed, that [same one] <u>will give life to the dead</u>, and He is over all things competent.

~~~~~~~~~~~~~~~~

Job 12:9-10; John 5:26; 10:10; 11:25; 1 Timothy 6:13.
Fussilet 41:39.

59

El-Muksit: (86)

(The Equitable)
(The Observer of Justice)
(The Fair One)
He deals with all on an equal basis.

Psalm 98:9 - Before the LORD; for he cometh to judge the earth: with righteousness shall <u>he judge the world, and the people with equity</u>.

James 3:17 - But the wisdom that is from above is first pure, then peaceable, gentle, *and* easy to be intreated, full of mercy and good fruits, <u>without partiality</u>, and without hypocrisy.

Al-i İmran 3:18 - He is <u>the upholder of Justice</u>. There is no deity save Him, The Almighty, the Wise.

~~~~~~~~~~~~~~~

Genesis 18:25; Proverbs 17:26; Isaiah 30:18; Romans 2:27.
Maide 5:42; A'raf 7:29; Enbiya 21:47.

60

El-Mu'id: (59)

(The Restorer)
(The Reproducer)
He rebuilds and restores all things.

Psalm 23:3 – <u>He restoreth my soul</u>: he leadeth me in the paths of righteousness for his name's sake.

Matthew 3:9 – And think not to say within yourselves, We have Abraham to *our* father: for I say unto you, that <u>God is able of these stones to raise up children unto Abraham</u>.

Buruj 85:13 – Indeed, it is <u>He who originates [creation]</u> and repeats.

~~~~~~~~~~~~~~~

Ruth 4:14-15; Isaiah 1:26; 57:15-19; Jeremiah 27:22; 30:17;
Joel 2:25; Matthew 3:9; Luke 6:10; Romans 11:23;
2 Corinthians 1:9; 5:17.
Yunus 10:4, 34; Neml 27:64; Ankebut 29:19.

61

El-Mu'iz: (24)

(The Honorer)
(The One Who Gives Honor)
(The Bestower of Honor)
He honors or abases whom He will.

1 Samuel 2:7 – <u>The LORD</u> maketh poor, and maketh rich: <u>he</u> bringeth low, and <u>lifteth up</u>.

Matthew 23:12 – And whosoever shall exalt himself shall be abased; and he that shall humble himself <u>shall be exalted</u>.

———

Al-i İmran 3:26 – Say, "O Allah, Owner of Sovereignty, You give sovereignty to whom You will and You take sovereignty away from whom You will. <u>You honor whom You will and You humble whom You will</u>. In Your hand is [all] good. Indeed, You are over all things competent."

~~~~~~~~~~~~~~~

1 Samuel 2:30; 1 Chronicles 29:11-12; Psalm 84:11; 147:6; Ezekiel 21:26; John 12:26; Romans 2:9-11.

62

El-Mujib: (44)

(The Responder)
(The Assenter)
He answers prayers when his servants call.

Exodus 22:23 – If thou afflict them in any wise, and they cry at all unto me, <u>I will surely hear their cry</u>.

1 John 5:14-15 – (14) if we ask any thing according to his will, <u>he heareth us</u>: (15) And if we know that he hear us, whatsoever we ask, <u>we know that we have the petitions that we desired of him</u>.

Hud 11:61 – Ask forgiveness of Him and then repent to Him. Indeed, <u>my Lord is near and responsive</u>.

~~~~~~~~~~~~~~~

2 Chronicles 7:13-15; Psalm 34:15, 17; Isaiah 65:24; Jeremiah 33:3; John 14:13-14; 16:23-24; Romans 10:12-13; James 1:5; 1 John 3:22.

63

El-Mukaddim: (71)

(The Expediter)
(The Promoter)
(The Forerunner)
He moves forward what He wills
and delays what He wills.

Isaiah 52:12 – For ye shall not go out with haste, nor go by flight: for the LORD will go before you; and <u>the God of Israel *will be* your rear guard</u>.

Hebrews 6:20 – Whither <u>the forerunner</u> is for us entered, *even* Jesus, made an high priest.

Nahl 16:61 – And if Allah were to impose blame on the people for their wrongdoing, He would not have left upon the earth any creature, but He defers them for a specified term. And when their term has come, <u>they will not remain behind an hour, nor will they precede [it]</u>.

~~~~~~~~~~~~~~

Exodus 13:21-22; Nehemiah 9:10-12; 1 Timothy 6:15.
Kaf 50:28.

64

El-Mukit: (39)

(The Sustainer)
(The Nourisher)
(The Maintainer)
He provides food for His creation.

Psalm 145:15-16 – (15) The eyes of all wait upon thee; and thou givest them their meat in due season. (16) <u>Thou</u> openest thine hand, and <u>satisfiest the desire of every living thing</u>.

Philippians 4:19 – But <u>my God shall supply all your need</u> according to his riches in glory by Christ Jesus.

Nisa 4:85 – Whoever intercedes for a good cause will have a reward therefrom; and whoever intercedes for an evil cause will have a burden therefrom. And <u>ever is Allah, over all things, a Keeper</u>.

~~~~~~~~~~~~~~~~

Genesis 2:15-16; 6:21; Job 38:41; Psalm 78:17-25; 104:10-15; 136:25; 146:7; Matthew 6:31-33; John 6:35.

65

El-Muktedir: (70)

(The Dominant)
(The Determiner)
(The Creator of All Power)
(The All-Authoratative One)
He prevails over enemies.

Isaiah 42:13 – The LORD shall go forth as a mighty man, he shall stir up jealousy like a man of war: he shall cry, yea, roar; <u>he shall prevail against his enemies</u>.

1 Timothy 6:15 – Which in his times he shall shew, *who is* <u>the blessed and only Potentate</u>, the King of kings, and Lord of lords;

Kamer 54:42 – They denied Our signs, all of them, so <u>We seized them with a seizure</u> of one Exalted in Might and <u>Perfect in Ability</u>.

~~~~~~~~~~~~~~~

1 Samuel 2:6-10; Jeremiah 1:17-19; 15:20-21; 20:11; Matthew 16:18-19; 28:18-20; Colossians 2:15.
Kehf 18:45; Kamer 54:55.

66

El-Mu'min: (6)

(The Faithful)
(The One Who Gives Security)
(The Inspirer of Faith)
He grants security to His servants.

Deuteronomy 7:9 – Know therefore that the LORD thy God, he is God, <u>the faithful God</u>, which keepeth covenant and mercy with them that love him and keep his commandments to a thousand generations.

Hebrews 12:2 – Looking unto Jesus, the author and <u>finisher of our faith</u>.

Hashr 59:23 – He is Allah, other than whom there is no deity, the King, the Holy, the All-Peaceable, <u>the Bestower of Faith</u>, the Overseer, the Exalted in Might, the Compeller, the Superior. Exalted is Allah above whatever they associate with Him.

~~~~~~~~~~~~~~~

2 Timothy 2:13; Revelation 19:11.

67

El-Mumit: (61)

(The Death-giver)
(The Taker of Life)
(The Bringer of Death)
(The Causer of Death)
(The Destroyer)
He causes to die, just as He causes to live.

Deuteronomy 32:39 – See now that I, *even* I, *am* he, and *there is* no god with me: <u>I kill</u>, and I make alive; I wound, and I heal: neither *is there any* that can deliver out of my hand.

Revelation 1:18 – *I am* he that liveth, and was dead; and, behold, I am alive for evermore, Amen; and <u>have the keys of hell and of death</u>.

Hijr 15:23 – And indeed, <u>it is We who</u> give life and <u>cause death</u>, and We are the Inheritor.

~~~~~~~~~~~~~~~

1 Samuel 2:6; 2 Kings 5:7; Luke 12:5.
Bakara 2:28; Al-i İmran 3:156; A'raf 7:158; Hadid 57:2.

68

El-Muntekim: (81)

(The Avenger)
He will avenge all wrongs done.

Isaiah 1:24 – Therefore saith the Lord, the LORD of hosts, the mighty One of Israel, Ah, <u>I will ease me of mine adversaries, and avenge me of mine enemies</u>:

Luke 18:7-8 – (7) And <u>shall not God avenge his own elect</u>, which cry day and night unto him, though he bear long with them? (8) I tell you that <u>he will avenge them speedily</u>.

Sejde 32:22 – And who is more unjust than one who is reminded of the verses of his Lord; then he turns away from them? Indeed <u>We</u>, from the criminals, <u>will take retribution</u>.

~~~~~~~~~~~~~~~

Deuteronomy 32:35, 43; Psalm 18:47; 94:1; Hosea 1:4; Romans 3:5; 12:19; 2 Thessalonians 1:8; Revelation 6:9-11; 18:20. Rum 30:47.

69

El-Musavvir: (13)

(The Designer)
(The Shaper of Beauty)
(The Flawless Fashioner)
(The Bestower of Form)
He fashions His creatures how He pleases.

Isaiah 45:18 – For thus saith <u>the LORD that created the heavens</u>; God himself that formed the earth and made it; he hath established it, he created it not in vain, <u>he formed it</u> to be inhabited: I *am* the LORD; and *there is* none else.

Romans 9:20 – Nay but, O man, who art thou that repliest against God? Shall the thing formed say to <u>him that formed it</u>, Why hast thou made me thus?

Mulk 67:3 – [And] <u>who created seven heavens in layers</u>.

~~~~~~~~~~~~~~~

Genesis 2:7-8, 19; Psalm 90:2; Isaiah 44:24.
Hashr 59:24.

70

El-Mute'ali: (78)

(The Exalted)
(The Highest Supreme One)
He has set Himself on high above all.

Isaiah 57:15 – For thus saith the high and lofty One that inhabiteth eternity, whose name *is* Holy; I dwell in the high and holy place, with him also *that is* of a contrite and humble spirit.

Luke 1:32 – He shall be great, and shall be called the Son of the Highest: and the Lord God shall give unto him the throne of his father David.

Ra'd 13:9 – [He is] Knower of the unseen and the witnessed, the Grand, the Exalted.

~~~~~~~~~~~~~~~

Genesis 14:22; Deuteronomy 10:17; 32:8; 1 Chronicles 16:31; 29:11; Psalm 147:5; Isaiah 55:8-9; 57:7, 15; Luke 1:35, 76; John 1:14; Acts 7:48; Hebrews 1:3, 8.

71

El-Mutekebbir: (10)

(The Proud)
(The Greatest)
He is supreme in majesty, sharing no
attributes of His creatures.

Note: This attribute is contra-indicated in the Bible since God sees, hears, gets angry; and He is not proud but humble and opposed to the proud. God hates pride!

Proverbs 6:16-17 – (16) These six *things* doth the LORD hate ... (17) A proud look.

James 4:6 – God resisteth the proud, but giveth grace unto the humble.

Hashr 59:23 – He is Allah, besides whom there is no other god ... The All-Powerful, the Proud!

Hadid 57:23 – Allah loves not the haughty, the vainglorious.

~~~~~~~~~~~~~~~

Psalm 101:5; Proverbs 16:18; 21:4; Matthew 11:29.
Nisa 4:36, 172-173; Lokman 31:18; Zumar 39:60, 72.

72

El-Muzil: (25)

(The Humbler)
(The Debaser)
(The Humiliator)
He will degrade and abase those who
have worshipped false gods.

Ezekiel 21:26 – Thus saith the Lord GOD; Remove the diadem, and take off the crown: this shall not *be* the same: exalt *him that is* low, and <u>abase</u> him that is high.

James 4:6 – But he giveth more grace. Wherefore he saith, <u>God resisteth the proud</u>, but giveth grace unto the humble.

Al-i İmran 3:26 – Say, "O Allah, Owner of Sovereignty, You give sovereignty to whom You will and You take sovereignty away from whom You will. You honor whom You will and <u>You humble whom You will</u>."

~~~~~~~~~~~~~~~~

Job 40:11-12; Daniel 4:37; Luke 4:11; James 1:9-10.
Yunus 10:28-29.

73

En-Nafi': (92)

(The Blesser)
He adds benefits and blessings to life.

Deuteronomy 28:1-2, 13 – (2) All these blessings shall come on thee, and overtake thee, if thou shalt hearken unto the voice of the LORD thy God. (13) And the LORD shall make thee the head, and not the tail; and thou shalt be above only, and thou shalt not be beneath; if that thou hearken unto the commandments of the LORD thy God, which I command thee this day, to observe and to do *them*:

Acts 3:26 – God, having raised up his Son Jesus, sent him to bless you, in turning away every one of you from his iniquities.

Rum 30:37 – Allah enlarges the provision for whom he wills, and straightens it (*for whom he wills*).

~~~~~~~~~~~~~~

Psalm 107:31-38; Proverbs 10:22; John 10:10; Hebrews 6:7, 14. Enbiya 21:66.

74

En-Nur: (93)

(The Light)
He illuminates both heaven and earth.

Isaiah 60:19 – The sun shall be no more thy light by day; neither for brightness shall the moon give light unto thee: but the LORD shall be unto thee an <u>everlasting light</u>, and thy God thy glory.

John 8:12 – Then spake Jesus … I am the light of the world … the light of life.

Nur 24:35 – <u>Allah is the Light of the heavens and the earth</u>. The example of His light is like a niche within which is a lamp, the lamp is within glass, the glass as if it were a pearly [white] star lit from [the oil of] a blessed olive tree, neither of the east nor of the west, whose oil would almost glow even if untouched by fire. <u>Light upon light</u>.

~~~~~~~~~~~~~~~~

John 9:5; 1 Timothy 6:15-16; James 1:17; 1 John 1:5; Revelation 21:23.

75

Er-Rafi: (23)

(The Exalter)
(The One Who Exalts His People)
He exalts some while He humbles others.

1 Samuel 2:7-8 – (7) The LORD maketh poor, and <u>maketh rich</u>: he bringeth low, and <u>lifteth up</u>. (8) He raiseth up the poor out of the dust, *and* lifteth up the beggar from the dunghill, to set them among princes, and to make them inherit the throne of glory:

James 1:9 – Let the brother of low degree rejoice in that he is <u>exalted</u>:

———

En'am 6:83 – And that was Our [conclusive] argument which We gave Abraham against his people. <u>We raise by degrees whom We will</u>. Indeed, your Lord is Wise and Knowing.

~~~~~~~~~~~~~~

Job 5:8-11; Ezekiel 21:26; Luke 14:11.
Mumin 40:15; Vakia 56:3.

76

Er-Rahim: (2)

(The Merciful)
(The All-Beneficent)
He is merciful especially to those who show mercy.

Psalm 111:4 – He hath made his wonderful works to be remembered: the LORD *is* gracious and full of compassion.

Psalm 145:8 – The LORD is gracious, and full of compassion; slow to anger, and of great mercy.

Romans 9:15 – For he saith to Moses, I will have mercy on whom I will have mercy, and I will have compassion on whom I will have compassion.

Fatiha 1:1 – In the name of Allah, the Entirely Merciful, the Especially Merciful.

~~~~~~~~~~~~~~

Lamentations 3:22; Matthew 9:36.
Bakara 2:37, 128, 143; Hajj 22:20; Hashr 59:22.

77

Er-Rahmân: (1)

(The Compassionate)
(The Most Gracious)
(The Beneficent)
He is gentle and full of compassion.

Exodus 34:6-7 – (6) And the LORD passed by before him, and proclaimed, The LORD, <u>The LORD God, merciful and gracious</u>, longsuffering, and abundant in goodness and truth, (7) <u>Keeping mercy for thousands</u>, forgiving iniquity.

Ephesians 2:4 – But God who is rich in mercy, for his great love wherewith he loved us.

Yusuf 12:64 – He said, "Should I entrust you with him except [under coercion] as I entrusted you with his brother before? But <u>Allah</u> is the best guardian, and <u>He is the most merciful of the merciful</u>."

~~~~~~~~~~~~~~~

Psalm 52:8; Psalm 145:8; Micah 7:19; Mark 1:4;
2 Corinthians 1:3.
Fatiha 1:1-2; Taha 20:8.

78

Er-Rakib: (43)

(The Watchful)
(The Observer)
He keeps watch over His creation so
that nothing is absent from Him.

Job 28:24 – For he <u>looketh</u> to the ends of the earth, *and* <u>seeth</u> under the whole heaven.

Job 34:21 – For his eyes are upon the ways of man, and <u>he seeth</u> all his goings.

Matthew 6:4 – That thine alms may be in secret: and thy Father which <u>seeth</u> in secret himself shall reward thee openly.

Maide 5:117 – Worship Allah, my Lord and your Lord. You were <u>the Observer</u> over them, and You are, over all things, <u>Witness</u>.

~~~~~~~~~~~~~~~

Genesis 31;49; 2 Chronicles 16:9; Psalm 33:13-15; Proverbs 5:21; Jeremiah 23:24; 31:28; John 16:30; 1 John 3:20. Nisa 4:1; Ahzab 33:52.

79

Er-Ra'uf: (83)

(The Kind)
(The Gentle)
(The Clement)
He is compassionate and merciful to His own.

Psalm 86:15 – But thou, O Lord, *art* a <u>God full of compassion</u>, and gracious, longsuffering, and <u>plenteous in mercy</u> and truth.

Matthew 14:14 – And Jesus went forth, and saw a great multitude, and was moved with <u>compassion</u> toward them, and he healed their sick.

Bakara 2:143 – And indeed, it is difficult except for those whom Allah has guided. And never would Allah have caused you to lose your faith. Indeed Allah is, to the people, <u>Kind and Merciful</u>.

~~~~~~~~~~~~~~~

Psalm 111:4; 145:8; Isaiah 49:15; Jeremiah 12:15; Mark 8:2; Romans 9:15; Hebrews 5:2.
Al-i İmran 3:30; Tevbe 9:117; Nahl 16:7; Hajj 22:65.

80

Er-Reshid: (98)

(The Orthodox)
(The Guide)
(The Righteous Teacher)
He leads and directs believers towards the right path.

Isaiah 48:17 – Thus saith the LORD, thy Redeemer, the Holy One of Israel; I *am* the LORD thy God which teacheth thee to profit, which leadeth thee by the way *that* thou shouldest go.

Luke 1:76-79 – (76) And thou, child, shalt be called the prophet of the Highest ... (79) to guide our feet into the way of peace.

Kehf 18:10 – [Mention] when the youths retreated to the cave and said, "Our Lord, grant us from Yourself mercy and prepare for us from our affair right guidance."

~~~~~~~~~~~~~~~~

Psalm 23:25:9; 32:8; 48:14; Isaiah 42:16; 58:11; Luke 12:11-12; John 16:13; 1 John 2:26-27.
Kehf 18:24.

81

Er-Rezzak: (17)

(The Provider)
(The Sustainer)
He dispenses daily food but asks no provision.

Psalm 136:25 – Who <u>giveth food</u> to all flesh: for his mercy *endureth* for ever.

John 6:35 – And Jesus said unto them, I am the bread of life: he that cometh to me shall <u>never hunger</u>; and he that believeth on me shall <u>never thirst</u>.

Philippians 4:19 – But my <u>God shall supply all your need</u> according to his riches in glory by Christ Jesus.

Dhariyat 51:58 – Indeed, it is Allah who is the [continual] <u>Provider</u>, the firm possessor of strength.

~~~~~~~~~~~~~~~

Genesis 2:15-16; Deuteronomy 2:7; 10:17-18; Psalm 23:1; 78:17-25; Matthew 6:31-33; Luke 12:22-24.

82

Es-Sabur: (99)

(The Patient)
(The Forbearing One)
He is very patient and slow to punish.

Exodus 34:6-7 – (6) The LORD, The LORD God, merciful and gracious, <u>longsuffering</u>, and abundant in goodness and truth, (7) Keeping mercy for thousands, forgiving iniquity and transgression and sin.

Psalm 103:8 – The LORD is merciful and gracious, <u>slow to anger</u>, and plenteous in mercy.

2 Peter 3:9 – The Lord is not slack concerning his promise, as some men count slackness; but is <u>longsuffering</u> to us-ward, not willing that any should perish, but that all should come to repentance.

Note: This attribute is not used of God in the Qur'an.

~~~~~~~~~~~~~~~

Psalm 86:15; 103:8; Romans 2;4.

83

Es-Samed: (68)

(The Eternal)
(The Satisfier of All Needs)
(The Supreme Provider)
He is impenetrable and independent of His creation.

Deuteronomy 33:27 – The <u>eternal God *is thy* refuge</u>, and underneath *are* the everlasting arms:

Psalm 46:1 – God *is* our refuge and strength, a very present <u>help in trouble</u>.

Romans 1:20 – For the invisible things of him from the creation of the world are clearly seen, being understood by the things that are made, even his <u>eternal power and Godhead</u>; so that they are without excuse.

———

Ikhlas 112:2 – Allah, the <u>Eternal Refuge</u>.

~~~~~~~~~~~~~~~

Psalm 9:9; 46:7, 11; 57:1; 59:16-17; 62:7-8; 91:2, 9;
1 Timothy 1:17; Hebrews 13:8.

84

Es-Selam: (5)

(The Peace)
(The Source & Maker of Peace)
(The Bestower of Peace)
His name is Peace.

Isaiah 9:6 – For unto us a child is born, unto us a son is given: and the government shall be upon his shoulder: and his name shall be called Wonderful, Counsellor, The mighty God, The everlasting Father, <u>The Prince of Peace</u>.

2 Thessalonians 3:16 – Now the <u>lord of Peace</u> himself give you peace.

Hashr 59:23 – He is Allah, other than whom there is no deity, the King, the Holy, <u>the All-Peaceable</u>, the Bestower of Faith, the Overseer, the Exalted in Might, the Compeller, the Superior. Exalted is Allah above whatever they associate with Him.

~~~~~~~~~~~~~~~

Psalm 29:11; Isaiah 26:3; 45:7; 1 Corinthians 14:33; Galatians 5:22; Ephesians 2:14.

85

Es-Semi: (26)

(The Hearer)
He sees and hears all things.

Psalm 94:9 – He that planted the ear, <u>shall he not hear</u>? he that formed the eye, shall he not see?

John 9:31 – Now we know that <u>God heareth</u> not sinners: but if any man be a worshipper of God, and doeth his will, him <u>he heareth</u>.

1 John 5:14 – And this is the confidence that we have in him, that, if we ask any thing according to his will, <u>he heareth us</u>.

En'am 6:13 – And to Him belongs that which reposes by night and by day, and <u>He is the Hearing</u>, the Knowing.

~~~~~~~~~~~~~~~

Exodus 22:23, 27; Psalms 4:3; Proverbs 15:29; Mathew 21:22; Hebrews 4:13.
Bakara 2:127, 137, 256; Nisa 4:158; Enfal 8:17; Isra 17:1; Hujurat 49:1.

86

Esh-Shahid: (50)

(The Witness)
He is witness to everything and from whom nothing is hidden.

Job 16:19 – Also now, behold, my witness *is* in heaven, and my record *is* on high.

1 John 5:9 – If we receive the witness of men, the witness of God is greater: for this is the witness of God which he hath testified of his Son.

Maide 5:117 – I said not to them except what You commanded me – to worship Allah, my Lord and your Lord. And I was a witness over them as long as I was among them; but when You took me up, You were the Observer over them, and You are, over all things, Witness.

~~~~~~~~~~~~~~~~

Psalm 33:13-15; Jeremiah 23:24; Hebrews 4:13; Revelation 1:5; 3:14.
Hajj 22:17; Sebe 34:47.

87

Esh-Shekur: (35)

(The Thankful)
(The Appreciative)
(The Rewarder of Thankfulness)
He graciously accepts and rewards
the service of His people.

Psalm 19:8-11 – (8) The statutes of the LORD *are* right ... (11) in keeping of them <u>*there is* great reward</u>.

Revelation 22:12 – And, behold, I come quickly; and <u>my reward *is* with me</u>, to give every man according as his work shall be.

Fatir 35:30, 34 – (30) That He may <u>give them in full their rewards</u> and increase for them of His bounty. Indeed, He is Forgiving and <u>Appreciative</u>. (34) And they will say, "Praise to Allah, who has removed from us [all] sorrow. Indeed, <u>our Lord *is*</u> Forgiving and <u>Appreciative</u>."

~~~~~~~~~~~~~~~

Luke 6:35; 1 Corinthians 3:8; Hebrews 6:10; 10:35; 11:6.
Shura 42:23; Taghabun 64:17.

88

Et-Tevvab: (80)

(The Repentant)
(The Relenting)
(The Guide to Repentance)
He turns from judgment and happily forgives.

Joel 2:12-14 – (12) Therefore also now, saith the LORD, <u>turn ye *even* to me with all your heart, and with fasting, and with weeping, and with mourning:</u> (13) And <u>rend your heart, and not your garments, and turn unto the LORD your God: for he is gracious and merciful, slow to anger, and of great kindness, and repenteth him</u> of the evil. (14) Who knoweth *if* he will return and <u>repent</u>.

Bakara 2:37 – Then Adam received from his Lord [some] words, and He accepted his repentance. Indeed, it is He who is the <u>Accepting of repentance</u>, the Merciful.

~~~~~~~~~~~~~~~~

Exodus 32:14; 2 Samuel 24:16; 1 Chronicles 21:15; Acts 5:31; 10:43.

89

El-Vahid: (66)

(The Unique)
He is without a partner in His divine sovereignty.

Isaiah 46:9-10 – (9) I am God, and *there is* none else; *I am* <u>God</u>, and *there is* <u>none like me</u>, (10) Declaring the end from the beginning, and from ancient times *the things* that are not *yet* done, saying, My counsel shall stand, and I will do all my pleasure.

John 10:30 – I and my Father are <u>one</u>.

John 14:9 – Jesus saith … he that hath <u>seen me hath seen the Father</u>.

Sad 38:65 – Say, [O Muhammad], "I am only a warner, and there is not any deity except Allah, <u>the One</u>, the Prevailing."

~~~~~~~~~~~~~~~~

Exodus 3:14; Deuteronomy 4:35, 39; 6:4-5; Isaiah 43:10-12; Mark 12:29-30; John 17:3.
Bakara 2:163; Nisa 4:171; Ra'd 13:16; Zumar 39:4; Mu'min 40:16.

90

El-Vajid: (64)

(The Discoverer)
(The Great Inventor)
He perceives and finds out all.

Jeremiah 23:24 – Can any hide himself in secret places that I <u>shall not see him</u>? saith the LORD. Do not I fill heaven and earth? saith the LORD.

Matthew 10:29-30 – (29) Are not two sparrows sold for a farthing? And one of them shall not fall on the ground <u>without your Father</u>. (30) But the very hairs of your head are all numbered.

Taha 20:115 – And We had already taken a promise from Adam before, but he forgot; and <u>We found not in him</u> determination.

~~~~~~~~~~~~~

Job 37:16; Psalm 33:13-15; 139:7-12, 15-16; 147:4-5;
Jeremiah 23:24; Amos 9:2-4; Hebrews 4:13; 1 John 3:20
Hebrews 12:2.
Sad 38:44; Duha 93:6-7.

91

El-Vali: (77)

(The Governor)
(The Protecting Friend)
He governs over His own.

Isaiah 9:6 – For unto us a child is born, unto us a son is given: and <u>the government shall be upon his shoulder</u>: and his name shall be called Wonderful, Counsellor, The mighty God, The everlasting Father, The Prince of Peace.

Matthew 2:6 – And thou Bethlehem ... out of thee shall come <u>a Governor</u>, that shall rule my people Israel.

Ra'd 13:11 – For each one are successive [angels] before and behind him who protect him by the decree of Allah. Indeed, Allah will not change the condition of a people until they change what is in themselves. And when Allah intends for a people ill, there is no repelling it. And there is <u>not for them besides Him any patron</u>.

~~~~~~~~~~~~~~~

Psalm 22:28; Psalm 146:10; Micah 5:2; Luke 1:32-33.
Nisa 4:45, 47.

92

El-Varis: (97)

(The Inheritor)
(The Supreme Heir)
All things will return to Him.

Psalm 2:8 – Ask of me, and I shall give thee the heathen for thine <u>inheritance</u>, and the uttermost parts of the earth *for* thy possession.

Colossians 1:15-16 – (15) Who is the image of the invisible God, the firstborn of every creature: (16) For <u>by him</u> were all things created, that are in heaven, and that are in earth, visible and invisible, whether *they* be thrones, or dominions, or principalities, or powers: all things were created by him, and <u>for him</u>.

Meryem 19:40 – Indeed, it is We who will <u>inherit</u> the earth and whoever is on it, and to Us they will be <u>returned</u>.

~~~~~~~~~~~~~~~

1 Corinthians 15:28; Hebrews 1:2-3, 11.
Al-i Imran 3:180; Hijr 15:23.

93

El-Vasi: (45)

(The Omnipresent)
(The All-Comprehending)
(The Vast and Boundless)
(The All-Embracing)
He encompasses and contains all things.

Jeremiah 23:23-24 – (23) *Am* I a God <u>at hand</u>, saith the LORD, and not a God afar off? (24) ... Do not <u>I fill heaven and earth</u>? Saith the Lord.

Colossians 1:15-17 – (17) And he is <u>before all things</u> and by him all things consist.

Bakara 2:115 – And to Allah belongs the east and the west. So wherever you [might] turn, there is the Face of Allah. Indeed, <u>Allah is all-Encompassing</u> and Knowing.

~~~~~~~~~~~~~~~

Psalm 34:7; 103:112; Jeremiah 5:22; Hebrews 1:3;
1 Corinthians 15:27-28.
Bakara 2:261, 268; Al-i Imran 3:73; Nisa 4:130; Nur 24:32.

94

El-Vedud: (47)

(The Loving)
He is compassionate and loving to His servants.

Jeremiah 31:3 – The LORD hath appeared of old unto me, *saying*, Yea, I have loved thee with an everlasting love: therefore with lovingkindness have I drawn thee.

1 John 4:7-8, 16 – (7) Beloved, let us love one another: for love is of God; and every one that loveth is born of God, and knoweth God. (8) He that loveth not knoweth not God; for God is love. (16) God is love.

———————

Hud 11:90 – Ask forgiveness of your Lord and turn to him (in repentance). For my Lord is indeed Merciful, Loving.

~~~~~~~~~~~~~~~

Hosea 2:19-23; 11:1, 4; Isaiah 43:4; 63:9; John 3:16; 13:34; 15:12; 16:27; 1 John 4:7-16; Revelation 1:5.
Buruj 85:14.

95

El-Vehhab: (16)

(The Bestower)
(The Giver of All)
He liberally and freely gives of His bounty.

Psalm 84:11 – For the LORD God *is* a sun and shield: the <u>LORD will give grace and glory</u>: no good *thing* will he withhold from them that walk uprightly.

James 1:5 – If any of you lack wisdom, let him ask of <u>God</u>, that <u>giveth to all *men* liberally</u>, and upbraideth not; and it shall be given him.

Sad 38:35 – He said, "My Lord, forgive me and grant me a kingdom such as will not belong to anyone after me. Indeed, You are the <u>Bestower</u>."

~~~~~~~~~~~~~~~~

Psalm 37:4; Ecclesiastes 2:26; Matthew 7:7-11; 21:22; John 15:7; Romans 8:32; Revelation 21:6.
Al-i Imran 3:8; Sad 38:9.

96

El-Vekil: (52)

(The Advocate)
(The Ultimate Trustee)
(The Disposer of Affairs)
He pleads for and defends others.

Leviticus 17:11 – For the life of the flesh *is* in the blood: and I have given it to you upon the altar to make an atonement for your souls: for it *is* the blood that maketh an atonement for the soul.

1 John 2:1 – If any man sin, we have an advocate with the Father, Jesus Christ the righteous.

En'am 6:102 – That is Allah, your Lord; there is no deity except Him, the Creator of all things, so worship Him. And He is Disposer of all things.

~~~~~~~~~~~~~~~~

Isaiah 53:4-6, 11-12; John 14:6; Romans 3:21-26; 2 Corinthians 5:14-21; Hebrews 9:12-15, 22; 1 John 4:10. Nisa 4:131-132; Hud 1:12; Kasas 28:28.

97

El-Veli: (55)

(The Guardian)
(The Patron Friend)
(The Governor)
He protects the safety of His saints.

Isaiah 41:10 – Fear thou not; for I *am* with thee: be not dismayed; for I *am* thy God: I will strengthen thee; yea, I will help thee; yea, <u>I will uphold thee</u> with the right hand of my righteousness.

John 15:15 – I have called you <u>friends</u>; for all things that I have heard of my Father I have made known unto you.

A'raf 7:196 – Indeed, my <u>protector</u> is Allah, who has sent down the Book; and He is an ally to the righteous.

~~~~~~~~~~~~~~~

2 Chronicles 20:6-7; Luke 12:11-12.
Bakara 2:57, 107, 120; Al-i Imran 3:68; A'raf 7:155; Jathia 45:19.

98

Ez-Zahir: (75)

(The Perceptible)
(The Outward Manifest One)
He is everywhere and known by decisive proof.

Psalm 104:24 – O LORD, how <u>manifold</u> are thy works! in wisdom hast thou made them all: the earth is full of thy riches.

Romans 1:20 – For the invisible things of him from the creation of the world are <u>clearly seen</u>, being understood by the things that are made, *even* his eternal power and <u>Godhead</u>; so that they are without excuse:

Hadid 57:3 – He is the First and the Last, <u>the Ascendant</u> and the Intimate, and He is, of all things, Knowing.

~~~~~~~~~~~~~~

Isaiah 40:26, 28; John 1:1, 14; 2:11; 3:13, 31, 34; 4:25-26; 1 Corinthians 8:6; Ephesians 4:6; 1 Timothy 3:16; Hebrews 1:3.

99

Zül'-Jelal-i ve'l-Ikram: (85)

(Lord of Majesty and Honor)
All majesty and honor belongs to Him.

1 Chronicles 29:11 – Thine, O <u>LORD</u>, *is* the greatness, and the power, and <u>the glory</u>, and the victory, and <u>the majesty</u>: for all *that is* in the heaven and in the earth *is thine*; thine *is* the kingdom, O LORD, and thou art <u>exalted</u> as head above all.

Revelation 5:12 – Worthy is the Lamb that was slain to receive power, and riches, and wisdom, and strength, and <u>honour, and glory</u>, and blessing.

Rahman 55:27, 78 – (27) And there will remain the Face of your Lord, <u>Owner of Majesty and Honor</u>. (78) Blessed is the name of your Lord, Owner of Majesty and Honor.

~~~~~~~~~~~~~~~

Zechariah 14:9; Acts 2:36; 26:15.

The "Best Names of God" (Esmaül-Hüsna) Mentioned in the Qur'an

A'râf 7:180 – And to Allah belong <u>the best names</u>, so invoke Him by them. And leave [the company of] those who practice deviation concerning His names.

Isra 17:110 – Say, "Call upon Allah or call upon the Most Merciful. Whichever [name] you call - to Him belong <u>the best names</u>." And do not recite [too] loudly in your prayer or [too] quietly but seek between that an [intermediate] way.

Hashr 59:24 – He is Allah, the Creator, the Inventor, the Fashioner; to Him belong <u>the best names</u>. Whatever is in the heavens and earth is exalting Him. And He is the Exalted in Might, the Wise.

Taha 20:8 – Allah - there is no deity except Him. To Him belong <u>the best names</u>.

There are 16 additional names found in the Qur'an but which are not included among the 99 names listed in the Esmaül-Hüsna.

Allah: (God)
Deuteronomy 10:17 / Bakara 2:255.

El-Fatir: (The Re-Creator)
Revelation 21:5 / Shura 42:11.

El-Gafir: (The Pardoner)
Micah 7:18 / Mumin 40:3.

El-Galib: (The Victorious)
John 16:33 / Yusuf 12:21

El-Hallak: (The Creative One)
Revelation 21:5 / Yasin 36:81

El-İlah: (The Great God)
Deuteronomy 10:17 / Bakara 2:163

El-Kahir: (The Subjugator)
Philippians 3:21 / En'am 6:61

El-Kafi: (The Self-Sufficient One)
Acts 17:25 / Zumar 39:36

El-Karib: (The Near One)
Acts 17:27 / Hud 11:61

El-Mevla: (The Watcher)
Proverbs 15:3 / Muhammad 47:11

El-Mubin: (The Evident One)
Romans 1:19-20 / Maide 5:15

El-Muhit: (The All-Encompassing One)
Romans 8:38-39 / Fussilat 41:54

El-Mustean: (The Helper)
Psalm 46;1 / Yusuf 12:18

En-Nasir: (The Helper of His Own)
Psalm 23:4 / Nisa 4:45

Er-Rab: (The Lord)
Psalm 118:27 / Meryem 19:64-65

Esh-Shakir: (The Appreciative)
Luke 6:35 / Bakara 2:158

Index of References Quoted From the Bible

Genesis 2:7	61
Genesis 16:2	56
Genesis 18:25	4
Genesis 30:2	52
Exodus 3:14-15	45
Exodus 15:11	53
Exodus 22:23	65
Exodus 33:20	17
Exodus 34:6-7	24, 49, 80, 85
Leviticus 17:11	99
Deuteronomy 6:4	6
Deuteronomy 7:9	69
Deuteronomy 10:17	10, 46
Deuteronomy 28:1-2, 13	76
Deuteronomy 32:4	4
Deuteronomy 32:39	70
Deuteronomy 33:27	13, 86
Nehemiah 9:17	23
1 Samuel 2:7-8	64, 78
1 Samuel 2:30	50
2 Samuel 22:37	16
1 Chronicles 29:11	8, 102
Job 16:19	89
Job 28:24	26, 81
Job 31:4	60
Job 34:21	81
Psalm 2:8	95
Psalm 19:1	18
Psalm 19:8-11	90
Psalm 23:3	63

Psalm 24:1	51
Psalm 24:8	44
Psalm 25:8	19
Psalm 46:1	86
Psalm 47:2-3	43
Psalm 48:1	35
Psalm 48:14	27
Psalm 55:19	20
Psalm 84:11	98
Psalm 86:15	82
Psalm 94:9	88
Psalm 95:6	14
Psalm 96:13	30
Psalm 98:9	62
Psalm 103:2-3	5
Psalm 103:8	85
Psalm 104:24	101
Psalm 111:4	79
Psalm 116:7	47
Psalm 119:32	16
Psalm 121:5-8	29
Psalm 121:7-8	59
Psalm 136:25	84
Psalm 139:1-4	26
Psalm 139:4	9
Psalm 145:8	79
Psalm 145:15-16	67
Proverbs 6:16-17	74
Proverbs 8:18	25
Proverbs 15:6	58
Proverbs 18:10	55
Isaiah 1:24	71
Isaiah 6:3	48
Isaiah 9:6	87, 94
Isaiah 40:28	33
Isaiah 41:10	100
Isaiah 42:13	68
Isaiah 43:15	54
Isaiah 44:6	7, 21

Reference	Page
Isaiah 45:18	57, 72
Isaiah 46:9-10	92
Isaiah 48:17	83
Isaiah 49:26	11
Isaiah 52:12	66
Isaiah 57:15	73
Isaiah 60:19	77
Isaiah 66:18	38
Jeremiah 10:10	32, 37
Jeremiah 23:23-24	96
Jeremiah 23:24	15, 93
Jeremiah 31:3	97
Jeremiah 32:17	42, 39
Jeremiah 32:27	10, 39
Lamentations 3:33	20
Ezekiel 21:26	28, 75
Ezekiel 31:15	41
Daniel 2:20-21	31
Daniel 7:14	40
Daniel 12:2	12
Joel 2:12-14	91
Micah 5:2	13
Zechariah 9:9	34
Zechariah 14:9	6
Malachi 3:8-10	36
Matthew 2:6	94
Matthew 3:9	63
Matthew 6:4	81
Matthew 6:14-15	5
Matthew 10:29-30	93, 60
Matthew 14:14	82
Matthew 21:1-11	34
Matthew 23:12	28, 64
Matthew 24:31	38
Mark 5:7	8
Luke 1:32, 35	46, 73
Luke 1:35, 46-49	48
Luke 1:49	11
Luke 1:76-79	83

Luke 5:19-21	24
Luke 9:43	10
Luke 18:7-8	71
John 1:1-3	14
John 1:4	37
John 2:11	40
John 5:21	61
John 5:22	30
John 6:35	84
John 7:46	18
John 8:12	77
John 9:31	88
John 10:7-11	22
John 10:10	16
John 10:28	29
John 10:30	92
John 14:6, 17	32
John 14:9	92
John 15:15	100
John 16:13	27
John 18:36	54
John 21:17	9
Acts 1:24	26
Acts 2:27	48
Acts 3:14	4
Acts 3:15	37
Acts 3:26	76
Acts 16:6-7	52
Acts 26:8	12
Romans 1:20	86, 101
Romans 2:4	19, 34
Romans 9:15	79
Romans 9:20	72
Romans 11:22	20
Romans 14:12	36
1 Corinthians 2:8	53
2 Corinthians 5:14	39
2 Corinthians 5:17	18
Ephesians 2:4-7	25, 80

Reference	Pages
Philippians 4:19	58, 67, 84
Colossians 1:15-16	95, 96
2 Thessalonians 1:8	43
2 Thessalonians 2:6-7	56
2 Thessalonians 3:16	87
1 Timothy 1:17	51, 54
1 Timothy 2:5	6
1 Timothy 6:14-16	45
1 Timothy 6:15	68
1 Timothy 6:16	17
2 Timothy 4:18	59
Titus 2:11	49
Hebrews 1:1-2	14
Hebrews 4:13	9, 15
Hebrews 6:20	66
Hebrews 12:2	69
Hebrews 12:23	30
Hebrews 13:8	13
James 1:5	19, 47, 98
James 1:9	78
James 1:17	55
James 2:19	6
James 3:17	62
James 4:6	74, 75
2 Peter 2:16	41
2 Peter 3:9	85
1 John 2:1	99
1 John 4:7-8, 16	97
1 John 5:9	89
1 John 5:14-15	88, 65
Jude 1:25	31
Revelation 1:8, 17	7
Revelation 1:17-18	21, 70
Revelation 3:7-8	22
Revelation 4:11	33, 50, 57
Revelation 5:12	102
Revelation 19:5	35
Revelation 19:6	42, 44
Revelation 22:12	90

Index of References Quoted From the Qur'an

Fatiha 1:1	79
Bakara 2:37	91
Bakara 2:115	9, 96
Bakara 2:129	31
Bakara 2:143	82
Bakara 2:225	34
Bakara 2:245	41
Bakara 2:255	8, 10, 37
Bakara 2:267	25, 35
Al-i İmran 3:2	45
Al-i İmran 3:9	38
Al-i İmran 3:18	62
Al-i İmran 3:26	51, 64, 75
Nisa 4:85	67
Nisa 4:86	36
Nisa 4:131	58
Maide 5:117	81, 89
En'am 6:13	88
En'am 6:83	78
En'am 6:101	18
En'am 6:102	99
En'am 6:103	49
En'am 6:115	4
A'raf 7:196	100
Enfal 8:69	24
Hud 11:61	65
Hud 11:66	44
Hud 11:73	53
Hud 11:90	97
Yusuf 12:64	80

Ra'd 13:9	73
Ra'd 13:11	94
Ibrahim 14:10, 42	56
Hijr 15:23	70
Nahl 16:61	66
Kehf 18:10	83
Meryem 19:40	95
TaHa 20:73	13
TaHa 20:82	23
Hajj 22:7	12
Hajj 22:54	27
Hajj 22:60	5
Hajj 22:62	46
Nur 24:35	77
Neml 27:40	47
Rum 30:50	61
Rum 30:37	76
Sejde 32:22	71
Ahzab 33:34	26
Sebe 34:21	29
Sebe 34:26	22
Fatir 35:30, 34	90
Fatir 35:44	42
Ya Sin 36:12	60
Sad 38:35	98
Sad 38:65	92
Mu'min 40:16	43
Shura 42:12	16
Fetih 48:11	20
Dhariyat 51:58	55, 84
Tur 52:28	19
Kamer 54:42	68
Rahman 55:27	40, 102
Rahman 55:78	102
Vakia 56:1-3	28
Hadid 57:3	7, 17, 21, 101
Hadid 57:23	74
Mujadile 58:1	15
Hashr 59:23	11, 39, 54, 59, 69, 74, 87

Hashr 59:24	14, 33
Juma 62:1	48
Mulk 67:3	72
Hakka 69:1	32
Buruj 85:13	57, 63
Buruj 85:15	50
Tin 95:8	30
Ikhlas 112:1-2	6, 86

Meet the Author

Dan Wickwire was born in California in 1951 and grew up in the city of Bakersfield. His military service included three years in the U.S. army, during which he was trained as a medic, a paratrooper, and a Green Beret. He served a tour of duty as a combat medic in Vietnam.

Dan's education includes:
- Bakersfield College, earning an associate's degree in liberal arts.
- Multnomah School of the Bible, studying Bible, Hebrew, and Greek, and earning a bachelor's degree in theology.
- Columbia Graduate School of Bible & Missions, earning a master's degree in Bible.
- Summer Institute of Linguistics (SIL); University of Washington at Seattle; University of Texas at Arlington; and University of Oklahoma at Norman, studying linguistics. Dan earned a master's degree in linguistics at Pacific Western University.
- Ankara University in Ankara, Turkey, completing one year of doctoral studies in Islamics in the Department of Islamic Theology.

Dan is married to Devri and is the father of three sons: Derek Yekta, Andrew Nadir, and Peter Can. He is an ordained minister who served as a church planting missionary in Turkey for twenty-eight years. Dan and Devri currently reside in the Turkish Republic of Northern Cyprus.

Dan's books can be downloaded at:

danwickwire.com

* *100 Questions About the Bible and the Qur'an*, (in Turkish) 144 pages, 1st Ed. 2001, 2nd Ed. 2003; (in English) 1st Ed. 2003, 2nd Ed. 2004.

* *200 Questions About the Bible and the Qur'an*, 120 pages, 2014. Also available in: Albanian, Arabic, Azeri, Chinese, Dutch, English, Farsi, French, German, Kazak, Korean, Norwegian, Polish, Portuguese, Romanian, Russian, Spanish, and Turkish.

* *An Analytical Analysis of the Similarities and Differences Between the Qur'an and the Bible*, (in Turkish) 216 pages, 2007; (in English) 224 pages, 2007.

* *An Outline of Jihad in Islamic History*, 144 pages, 2015.

* *A Theological Sourcebook*, (in English) 240 pages, 1985; (in Turkish) 240 pages, 1987.

* *Has the Bible Been Changed?* (in Turkish) 48 pages, 1st Ed. 1987; 2nd Ed. 1994; 3rd Ed. 2007; 4th Ed. 2014; (in English) 96 pages, 1st Ed: 1987; 2nd Ed. 2007; 3rd Ed. 2011; 108 pages, 4th Ed. 2014.

* *The Reliability of the Scriptures According to Jewish, Christian and Islamic Sources*, (in Turkish only) 420 pages, 1999.

* *The Role of Prayer and Fasting in Binding and Loosing with Special Reference to the Problem of Reaching the Unreached People of the World Today*, unpublished thesis at Columbia, 78 pages, 1983.

* *The Sevmek Thesis: A Grammatical Analysis of the Turkish Verb System: Illustrated by the verb "Sevmek" = "To Love,"* published thesis (in English and Turkish), 170 pages, 1987; 2nd Ed. 1,000 pages, 2012.

* *The Wickwire Compendium of Islam*, 1,000 pages, 2010.

www.ingramcontent.com/pod-product-compliance
Lightning Source LLC
Chambersburg PA
CBHW070149080526
44586CB00015B/1907